J. B

Thanks for being a subscriber ... or thank your mother!

So many years of friendship now, much valued

My kindest regards

Dave B.

No beating about the Bush

No beating about the Bush

My final year: a teacher's Diary

David A Bush

edited by Roger Dowling

The Old Almondburians' Society

Published by
The Old Almondburians' Society
King James's School
Almondbury
HD4 6SG

Design: Roger Dowling
Jacket illustration: Charlie Starkey
Other illustrations: Roger Dowling
Typeset in EB Garamond

Print: Dolman Scott Ltd
1 High Street
Thatcham
Berkshire
RG19 3JG

ISBN 978 0 9557314 2 6

Also available from
The Old Almondburians' Society:

A History of King James's Grammar School in Almondbury (1963)
Gerald Hinchliffe

King James's School in Almondbury: An Illustrated History (2008)
Roger Dowling /John A Hargreaves (editors)

Morning Assembly (2012)
Andrew Taylor/Roger Dowling (editor)

All publications available online from
www.oas.org.uk

To my second wife, Margaret
who has always said that the school was my first

CONTENTS

AUTHOR'S NOTE

THIS Diary records my final year of teaching at King James's School at Almondbury, near Huddersfield in 1995-96. The idea of keeping a record of my final year of teaching was purely my own while that of having it published was the result of much pressure from my immediate family. I have reproduced it in almost all of its original form. It was never intended to be a literary masterpiece. However, I have resisted the temptation to make major alterations and improvements.

I decided it would be wiser to avoid mentioning colleagues, pupils and parents by name. The identity of the Senior Management Team – Clive Watkins (headteacher), Pat Reid (fellow deputy) and Jack Taylor (senior teacher) – is obvious, so there is no point in hiding it.

Short passages have also been omitted which were highly critical of certain colleagues and which would have caused them embarrassment. Teaching is such a tough job and it's inevitable that some manage it far better than others.

I am aware that these pages contain occasional criticism of Clive. Most of this emanates, I would suggest, from a clash of managerial styles. I wish to offset this by saying that Clive was one of the most hard-working and conscientious colleagues whom I have ever met. He was always a real gentleman and was always considerate. Add to the burden of running a school the fact that his wife was seriously ill during my final year and one realises what duress he was under. Not surprisingly, he had major heart surgery soon after I left and took premature retirement.

I should like to add a note about my fellow deputy, Pat. While I was the ostentatious one, Pat was comparatively quiet; but together we always worked in harmony and I believe we made a good team. Her dedication to the pupils' welfare was so much appreciated by so many. It was not surprising that she entered the Church of England Ministry on her retirement.

In the past 20 years, pressures in schools have increased tremendously, with the advent of mobile phones for all, Twitter, Facebook and similar social media . In addition, there is the prevalence of drugs in many schools.

I often wonder if I could have coped.

David A Bush
Porthcawl
November 2020

ACKNOWLEDGEMENTS

To all those who have subscribed to this book in its early stages, much gratitude; it gave my editor Roger Dowling and me confidence to carry on to publication.

I am most grateful to Andrew Taylor for contributing a Foreword. He was an outstanding student at King James's and went on to Oxford. I have maintained close links with Andrew over many years.

A special mention to the chairman of the Old Almondburians' Society, Walter Raleigh. Walter has been outstanding in his support for this enterprise and I am confident that he will be happy with the outcome.

Proofreading is a demanding task and for *No beating about the Bush* this was undertaken initially by Keith Crawshaw, one of the all-time greats among Old Almondburians and another pupil with whom I have retained a close friendship for 50 years. The final proofreading was carried out by my daughter Catherine Bonet, who has, I am happy to say, inherited her father's love of pedantry. I have had the final read-through so any remaining errors must be a case of *culpa mea*.

Thanks are also due to Old Almondburians Graham Cliffe and Richard Oughton who read the final text and offered valuable comments.

I was delighted that Robert Sutcliffe of the *Huddersfield Examiner* showed such an interest in the book and afforded it much publicity. It certainly brought in more subscribers.

Charlie Starkey, I clearly remember, showed outstanding talent in Art while at King James's. His career in that field in the USA has brought him Emmy awards and I am honoured that he was more than willing to design the jacket of my Diary.

No beating about the Bush would never have made it to the printing press were it not for the initial belief in it shown by my editor, Roger Dowling. His enthusiasm and commitment swept me along. He has spent hundreds of hours arranging the day-by-day account of my last year at KJS into its final form. Added to the basic text have been his sketches, photographs and explanatory notes. The finished product is, in my view, quite remarkable and I am humbly grateful to him. I should also express my thanks to his wife Judy for her patience as his dedication must have removed him over a long period from many domestic duties.

Finally, back to school. Here I acknowledge my debt to all those colleagues with whom I taught over so many years. Almost without exception we worked well together and their friendship and support kept me going when times were tough.

I have left the most important and sincere acknowledgement until last. It has to be of my former pupils and students. They have enriched my life beyond measure and if I have to varying degrees enriched theirs, then it has all been worthwhile.

EDITOR'S NOTE

IN order to retain the readability of the diary entries, redacted names are shown in the form of randomly chosen initials, thus: D——. These initials should not be construed as representing the initial of the person concerned. Throughout the book, Clive Watkins is referred to as 'Clive'; Jack Taylor as 'Jack' and Pat Reid as 'Pat'. Words inserted editorially are enclosed in square brackets.

Roger Dowling

FOREWORD

THIS is not the Dave Bush I remember.

Well, it wouldn't be, would it? I'm looking back over more than 50 years, to a time when I'm a fresh-faced little boy with bare knees, a school cap, and a shiny new leather satchel, and Dave Bush is – not that I realised this at the time – actually not that much different.

As form master of 1 Alpha (Alpha? Oh, go and look it up on that Google thing you keep telling me about), he was a big part of an awe-inspiring new world in which we had masters, not teachers – and masters who were called Sir, or you knew about it. There were no girls in those far-off, unenlightened days, and we were no longer the biggest boys in the school, but the smallest. We had break, never playtime; we had homework; we got lines, or detentions, and sometimes a clip round the back of the head, which no one found remarkable.

That's the boys, of course, not Mr Bush. He was called Twig behind his back (Bush – Twig, geddit?) and treated with a slightly nervous respect to his face. Instead of the grey shorts, he had sharply-creased grey flannel trousers, a dark blue Leeds University blazer, and shiny black shoes. Often, he wore a formal black gown, and sometimes, just sometimes, a broad smile. We learned quickly that you didn't mess around in his lessons.

But he, too, was at the start of a new adventure. 1 Alpha was his, as well as our, first form. He'd been at the school for only a couple of years – this was his first job after university. Before that, he'd had such a successful spell at King James's as a student teacher that the Headmaster had telephoned his tutor to suggest he should apply for a job on the staff in the English department.

Like us – though again, we had no idea of this – he had to watch his step. How his heart must have leapt into his mouth one summer morning when the Headmaster walked into one of his English lessons to find a boy sitting at the back with a radio, monitoring the score in the Test match. And how relieved he must have been when the Head, leaving a couple of minutes later, said quietly, "Hurrumph! Very good, Mr Bush. Bonding with the boys."

He was, in short, what I would call from today's perspective not much more than a boy himself. But his appointment, the Gaffer said privately many years later, was one of the best he had ever made.

Dave had, from the start, two talents that are invaluable to a teacher. The first was for being there when someone was doing something they shouldn't be – his pale blue Ford Anglia estate would appear as if by magic in St Helen's Gate when there was some rowdiness or fighting or smoking going on. He was the one who would walk round the corner when someone was amending the School notice board with some piece of witty graffiti. He was the nemesis of the Behind-The-Gardener's-Shed- Smoking-Club.

But his other gift was rarer and much more valuable: he could pass on his delight in what he was teaching like very few other teachers I've ever known. When we'd each worked our way through a few more years at school I remember the infectious enthusiasm with which he – teaching Sixth Form Latin now – would greet the exact right word that someone offered in a Latin 'unseen'. Picking through the work of Roman poets might be boring drudgery, but it never was.

His commitment and sense of purpose was wide ranging, and not always welcome to a small boy. Half way round the junior cross country course, when the runners were already miles ahead and the secret smokers hiding somewhere under a bridge a long way behind, you would be struggling up a steep hillside with the gate at the top lost in the distance, and stop to stagger a few paces at a walk. And there, in the distance, would appear that figure, in a smart three-quarter length overcoat. "Run! RUN!" And you gulped hard and ran.

It's that enthusiasm and commitment, more than anything, that survive in the Dave Bush whose day-to-day thoughts on his last year as Deputy Head at King James's are set down here. The School has changed several times, and in many ways, and he is older, wiser, and more immersed in the organisational challenges of a school of 750 pupils and more than 40 staff. Yes, there are the annoying issues such as graffiti in the toilets or nose studs in Year 8, and the serious and intractable problems that boys and girls suffer as they grow up, such as self-harming, or abuse at home.

Yes, there are times when he sounds tired and dispirited, worn down as any teacher must sometimes be by the apparent lack of interest from uninvolved and dysfunctional parents or the trials of Ofsted inspections and form-filling.

But there are also those moments when the joy and privilege of teaching shines through – the School dance evening, for instance, where the sheer excellence and dedication of the performers brings him to tears, or the unexpected achievements of boys or girls who have previously been known only for being in trouble.

The Gaffer, Dave Bush's early mentor and friend of many years, used to say that teaching was the best and most rewarding job in the world for anyone who loved it. For anyone who didn't, he would add, it could be a miserable hell on earth.

I was wrong in my first conclusion, of course. The Dave Bush who writes here at the end of his career is the same man I remember at the start of it – a man who loved teaching, and who inspired generations of boys and girls to do more and achieve more than they ever thought possible.

Andrew Taylor (King James's Grammar School 1963-70)
Bidford-on-Avon

KING JAMES'S SCHOOL

KING JAMES'S SCHOOL, as it is now known, is situated in an idyllic location in the Farnley Valley in Almondbury, an ancient village on the southern outskirts of Huddersfield in West Yorkshire.

Although officially the school dates from 1608 when it received its Royal Charter from King James I, its foundation is even older. Its origin was a chantry school located roughly 200 yards from its present site. This chapel was dismantled and rebuilt on the school's present site in 1547.

The school I originally joined in September 1961, as the latest of the 21 teaching staff, was King James's Grammar School, a very traditional two-stream school for boys. In the 1960s, the move towards comprehensive education was gathering momentum and the future of King James's was uncertain. Closure seemed a possibility. However, the Local Education Authority decided it should become a Sixth Form College, the result being that in September 1974, for the first time in 366 years, girls passed through King James's portals.

It soon became apparent that Huddersfield did not need three Sixth Form Colleges. The solution was to turn it into a 13-18 mixed comprehensive, drawing its pupils from the growing middle-class housing estates some distance from the school. Hence the buses which feature so frequently in this diary. September 1976 epitomises these 'years of change'.

The school then comprised the last of the Sixth Form College students (Year 13) in the Upper Sixth, no Lower Sixth (Year 12), the last of the grammar school boys in the fifth (Year 11), no fourth formers (Year 10) and the first 180 mixed ability boys and girls in the third form (Year 9). It is highly unlikely that this ludicrous situation has ever been replicated in any other educational institution in the UK. Even this new arrangement only lasted until 1990 when a final transformation turned King James's into an 11-16 school.

I fully expected that following my retirement, and that of other long-serving staff, King James's School would slide into inevitable decline. Such hubris! In fact, the school has continued to expand, is vastly oversubscribed and has an outstanding academic record.

Floreat Schola!

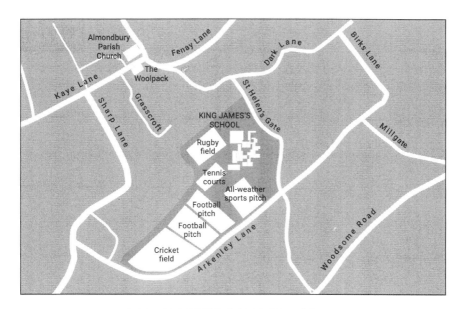

KING JAMES'S SCHOOL 1995/96

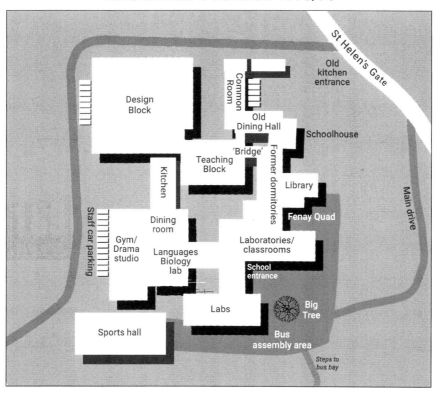

CHAPTER 1

September
1995

— The final year begins...

AUTUMN TERM

Monday 4th September 1995

191
DAYS TO GO

THE 35th year, the 103rd term begins. Beautiful morning, church clock strikes 8.00 am as I enter the school grounds. L—— is first into my room regarding his lost first day programme. Two references to write for last year's ITT[1] student teachers. First glimpse of staff. Are these [the same] sun-tanned, cheerful, chirpy souls those who left pale, worn and drawn last July?

Years 7 and 10 only in today. Year 7 bright and smart, wide-eyed but not overawed. Printing out individual timetables. What a contrast from the days of shouting out details to all in the dining room.

Extensive discussions with R—— and T—— over exam results analysis while others joined in in the staffroom. How pleased the governors would be to see us discussing how 199 'D's could have been turned into 'C's. What a change from the days of 1960s head Harry Taylor when exam results were dismissed in 30 seconds while arrangements for distribution of cutlery took up much time and raised certain staff's hackles.

Lengthy discussion over letter from Mrs C—— complaining about daughter's lower rather than upper sets in Year 10, ie unwilling to accept teachers' professional advice [despite being] herself a teacher. Complimentary letters from a resident in Grasscroft and the owner of Clough House, passed by some pupils on way to school, regarding their good behaviour and lack of litter; how much appreciated.

Management meeting where part-time teachers' hours to be reduced by not paying them for registration and assembly time. I protested. Undervaluing them will bring problems.

Old Almondburians' Society[2] meeting tonight. Old Almondburians' Cricket Club v school row over fees rumbles on[3].

[1] *Initial Teacher Training, required in the UK to become a qualified teacher*
[2] *A large fellowship of former pupils and staff of King James's School*
[3] *A grievance concerning the charges the school wished to introduce to enable the Old Almondburians' Society Cricket Club to use the cricket field*

Tuesday 5th September 1995

BAD night. Phone call at 10.00 pm from Old Almond-burian P—— , unhappy about the increased fees for use of Sports Hall for soccer training. Used to be free for Old Almondburians, now £400 per annum. This, plus OAS v School cricket field charges, meant 3.00 am rise and hot milk and aspirins. Spilt over into day with Clive and Bursar

First lesson Year 9 Latin. Difficult gearing up for another year. Will be OK when under way. Establishing routines is so important and time-consuming for both staff and pupils.

Year 11 following – usual chat about last year's results and 'only two-term year'. Annual reminder about rings, trainers, short skirts. Reported motorbike on premises during lunch time.

Bus duty at 3.10 pm brought a first in 35 years. Year 7 pupil arriving late for buses was told by DAB to queue, went berserk. Screamed "I'll miss my f****** bus," regularly repeated. Sat down and hurled bag to ground. When asked to give his name screamed his refusal. Other pupils calmly and commendably amused. Other colleagues equally calm but felt quite helpless. It was eventually decided to allow him to go down to bus bay as we dare not further tackle or restrain him. Great news for those in the staff room who found it all highly amusing.

Phone call to inform us that D—— was returning from the south. She left one year ago and was set to return north last Friday. Then father heard he was not to be relocated so she was devastated. So unhappy at present school. Mother returning to Grandma in Huddersfield next Monday.

End of day feeling tired and drained.

Wednesday 6th September 1995

The demented dervish of yesterday was in a very tearful state in reception area awaiting me. He was accompanied by his father. Time: 8.10 am. "He had missed his bus and run home," according to the father. "[He was] panic stricken. Said Mr Bush had shouted at him." The potentially aggressive father calmed down and changed dramatically when, supported by C——, the events of last night were made clear to him. I showed him personally the queue-ing arrangements. "Panic attack"was seized on by the father who is going to seek medical advice. The father ostensibly not very bright but appreciative.

The first lesson Latin with Year 8 and Classical Studies with Year 9. I enjoyed both lessons immensely, even though in Latin, for example, it was the 28th time I had started this course.

My reading of the imaginary register, "Ramsbottom, Arrowsmith..." backfired when I read out "Bartholomew" and a boy on the front row answered "Yes, Sir." Moral: check the real register first.

My timeline for Classical Studies was aided by the first girl I asked having a great-grandmother of 97.

The cricket club/ground hire [disagreement] coming to an end and Graham Cliffe is delighted with the latest arrangements. Thank goodness! Now for the footballers.

Bus duty was dull in comparison with yesterday. Year 7 pupil with nose stud "[It] will be out tomorrow." Year 9 pupil has the same for "cultural reasons". Clive to consult with fellow Heads.

Buses problem for Kirkheaton continues. Three double-deckers yes-terday morning, one double and one single this evening. The bus com-pany assured me two double-deckers tonight and three by next Monday. Generally a satisfying day although worries over some antagonism in the office continue.

Thursday 7th September 1995

CHILDREN mislead parents. Angry parent on the phone that Year 7 had been kept in late last night for five minutes by S——, thereby missing the Kirkheaton bus. Investigation re-vealed that the girl had been promptly released and had dawdled up the hill. Father to be informed.

Year 8 Latin (Spanish group) first lesson was a repeat of yesterday's but not nearly as good. Why? Unpredictable teacher's mood, late arrivals, lack of two chairs, all combine to change the atmosphere. Beginnings of lessons are so important. All ITA material arrived from Bretton [Hall College of Education][1] and the University of Huddersfield. Eight students due.

Saw A—— and spoke for first time this term offering a chat. Do I try to remain on friendly terms with all colleagues this year? Do I avoid confrontational situations?

With Clive and Pat at her house 11.30 am to 1.15 pm to discuss the management posts for 1st September 1996. Really dividing up my role. Redundancy would be financially very attractive but would also benefit the school financially, I believe. Also because any successor would inevitably be compared with me probably unfavourably initially. What hubris!

Beginning to consider colleague by colleague who has the potential/promise to fill various roles, and an excellent lunch. Back to school in torrential rain. How had school managed without its top three? Answer: most probably would be that they had not been missed.

MBWA[2] for the first time this term and generally all very quiet. Early days – the honeymoon period?

[1] *Bretton Hall College of Education opened as a teacher training college in 1949 with awards from the University of Leeds. It merged with the University of Leeds in 2001 and the campus closed in 2007.*

[2] *Management by walking around*

Friday 8th September 1995

TEACHING first four lessons but bombarded with Kirkheaton bus problems before the day really began. One Year 7 pupil, according to his mother, did not reach home before 5.45 pm. Years 10 and 11 stretching across the seats preventing smaller ones sitting down.

What a contrast in lessons one/two and three/four. One/two was lowest set Classical Studies. "Give me the name of a famous Roman, initials JC". Answer: "Jesus Christ". Three/four, Year 11 Latin discussing the finer points of the imperfect subjunctive in negative final clauses with the brightest pupil.

At break a phone call from a father concerned over Year 10 Preferences[1]. Wanted to take History instead of Art. The group originally was too large but one of them had dropped out. J—— was delighted to have him. Within three minutes, the changes had been made on the computer, a new personal timetable printed out and in the pupil's hand. Hope the father was impressed.

Should have mentioned that the two hours plus of Years 9 and 10 brought, as a result of a very intense teaching, that 'tight-under-the-ribs' feeling which is very draining. Colleagues are going on for double that time during a day; so demanding, and pacing is so important. No wonder teachers are drained at the end of the day, week, year, career.

Lunchtime saw that alarming feature of 'herding' as Clive puts it. Great masses of pupils charging around the buildings. Alarming for lunchtime supervisors and self to lesser extent. There is always the fear of a mob out of control or a child falling and a resultant accident.

Year 7 punched in the eye by another Year 7. Threats, rumours, tale-telling begin to surface regularly. It's Friday.

To Pat's house with Clive for planning next year's management and beyond.

[1]*At the end of Year 9 pupils opted for those subjects which they wished to study to GCSE level. These were called 'Preferences' or 'Options'.*

Monday 11th September 1995

WHAT a day! The honeymoon is most certainly over. If this were marriage then divorce could be just around the corner! One of those days when bombarded with queries, problems, telephone calls, it was difficult at times to keep one's cool, to cope and to prioritise. Began before 8.20 am when an angry Almondbury resident rang to complain that one of our pupils had verbally abused her in the village. I promised to investigate.

Bus trusties[1] revealed that Friday's Kirkheaton bus was one of the worst-ever evenings. Not two doubles as promised but one double and one single. Double had up to 50 standing according to one girl. So crammed on that Year 7s were screaming for fear of being crushed. Rang the bus company and expressed my white-hot rage. I stunned the *York-*

6

shire Rider man into silence. "Tonight three doubles"– later reduced to "two doubles and a single". We shall see.

Saw abuse-deliverer at 11.00 am: Year 10 girl. It was handled badly by me – far too much volume. Girl, however, reluctant to admit anything despite my seeing independently two others there at same time who confirmed her guilt. Finished up by her practically screaming defiance and leaving the premises. Father, or rather stepfather, rang at lunchtime. Generally supportive. I shall see girl tomorrow morning. Rang complainant and confirmed that action was being taken.

Lunchtime saw numerous miscreants sent by lunchtime supervisors – generally minor offences. How would they manage if all the staff left the premises? Management meeting 2.00 pm until 4.10 pm. So many day-to-day problems to discuss that major ones were being pushed to one side.

S—— had major problem with a pupil. He had threatened to shoot her. Not taken too seriously. As I left I heard that he had been found to have an airgun and pellets in his bag. More details tomorrow. Telephone messages left on the desk, until tomorrow.

[1] *Trusted informants*

Tuesday 12th September 1995

LOOKING in the mirror this evening at 5.00 pm I wondered where the relaxed, sun-tanned fellow of 10 days ago had disappeared to. Dark around the eyes, the worried frown returned. Yet not as hectic as yesterday.

The airgun and pellets incident is being dealt with by a planned visit from the Police Youth Liaison Officer. Clive seems determined to play it down while more militant staff want to build it up. "The Head will have his way."

Bridges have been repaired with yesterday's runaway. [Her] troubled background demands, or at least requires, sympathy but stronger action will have to be taken if there is a next time. A trying pupil in both senses of the word.

Lunchtime dominated by torrential downpour; a leaking roof over Dorm 1 resulted in: 'Emergency.' Building Services sent for.

Peter Heywood, former KJS science teacher/local artist arrived. He brought a commissioned painting of the school which had been done in memory of Mike Thornton, our recently departed Head of English[1]. Peter also brought news of his intended retirement at the age of 52. The photographer was an hour late for a special assembly. I was to introduce Peter but Clive stole most of my lines.

Phone calls from Martyn Hicks regarding OAS soccer problems. Janine King at Greenhead College[2] is setting up a GC/KJS student/pupil links arrangement. The deputy head at Almondbury High School is keen to share GCSE results. Almondbury are clearly closing the gap on us while I know Salendine Nook have performed very well.

Met with B—— and N—— to discuss results, statistics and future admissions limits.

Despite promises of three double-deckers last night only one double and two singles to Kirkheaton, I hear. Another phone call tomorrow.

Marked an outstanding set of Year 11 Latin Set books with work on 'The Roman House'. A very positive note on which to end the day.

[1]*Mike Thornton died on 23rd April 1995*
[2]*Sixth Form College in Huddersfield set up in 1974; formerly Greenhead High School for Girls*

Wednesday 13th September 1995

YAWNED very loudly and involuntarily in the office today. Halfway through the second week, as I said to the amused office staff. Felt very tired but awake at 4.00 am thinking about school matters and could not get back to sleep.

Generally a quieter day, although setting things up, getting pupils and self into a routine is very wearing. Arranging my chalk, board-cleaning, and 'five minutes to end of lesson' monitors in each class[1] is demanding. Yet I know it helps 'lesson-life' to run so much more smoothly as the year progresses.

Kirkheaton buses? Now up to two doubles and a single last night so my irate phone call was shelved temporarily.

The marking of one set of 32 books took some considerable time. With an extra group I shall have to cut down somehow, I suspect. Today's smile must be when R—— showed me some Year 7 exercise books which had brown paper sheets covering the back. They had followed his request literally by 'backing' their books.

Lunchtime meeting with English/Maths heads of teams and assistants discussing the introduction of IT[2] into the Year 7 teaching programme. Felt I did a really good job in chairing a meeting, the content of which was mostly outside my sphere of knowledge – and interest.

Noise at the end of the day outside M——'s room. One pupil on the outside while others inside blocking his entry. A bellow admitted me. This is a struggling teacher in the second year of her profession. I doubt she'll ever cope. How shall we manage? She really should seek another profession.

General atmosphere when doing some MBWA this afternoon was very well ordered.

[1]*In each class a pupil was appointed whose job it was to put up a hand and remind DAB there were five minutes left in the lesson, meaning that it was time to wind up and set homework.*
[2]*Information Technology*

Thursday 14th September 1995

A BUSY day. Really began at 8.15 am although I was in school by soon after 8.00 despite, thanks to *Nytol*[1], sleeping over by 20 minutes.

Two Year 11 girls came to report two Year 7s bullying another Year 7 especially on the bus – Kirkheaton again – and particularly unpleasant. I dealt with this during period one and lunchtime. There had been some provocation but loud threats regarding parents and exclusion should suffice this time.

In Briefing, Year 8 pupil now has no hearing problem as bits of rubbers have been removed from his ears. This made me think of our daughter Catherine and her Smurf's hat lodged in her ear from junior school to post teacher training year medical.

[There were] 35 in Year 8 Latin (Spanish group) lesson which went poorly compared with yesterday's German group equivalent. Why? Minor matters can so easily change the atmosphere.

9

Reports of Year 11 girl being thrown out of her home are upsetting as I remember her as a sweet, smiling 11-year-old to whom I taught English. How pupils change from 11 to 16! Physically so much but even more socially and temperamentally and it is so often caused by family circumstances. Some solid and supportive; others fractious and fragmented.

Lunchtime supervisors continue to send me a steady stream of 'offenders'. Rapid dispensation of justice needed.

Year 11 assembly Bible reading was on the theme 'A building founded on rock'. There was stress on maturity and more adult relationships with teachers. Half an hour later C—— brought me two Year 11s who were singing childishly and disobediently in the IT room, and reprimand for another Year 11 sent out by D—— for immature behaviour. So much for my assembly.

Pat and I joined the Unwind Club[1] in the staffroom 3.15 pm to 3.45 pm. It's so useful especially as I can pick up much gossip here and take the school's temperature.

[1]*A proprietaty diphenhydramine taken to relax and aid sleep.*
[2]*An informal gathering of teaching colleagues in the staffroom at the end of the day to discuss the day's events and share experiences*

Friday 15th September 1995

TWO weeks gone, approximately 36 to go. Although individual days may seem long, Friday to Friday passes surprisingly, alarmingly, reassuringly quickly depending on one's view. Five weeks to half term as someone remarked. Typical – teachers wishing their time away.

Today has passed comparatively smoothly for a Friday. Clive away yesterday afternoon and all day today so I was ultimately in charge or responsible for 750 pupils, 40+ staff, various auxiliaries, X million pounds of plant etc etc for a salary of just around £30,000 in my final year. How does that compare with similar experience and responsibility in industry?

I realise more and more that it is impossible to keep account of all events; even attempting to recall them in a notebook more or less as they occur doesn't work as one is swept from one matter to another. I recall yesterday's Year 11 pupil whom we discussed at lunchtime and his appeal for help. Showed Jack his arms cut by razor blades. "Nobody likes me. I want my psychologist again. Don't tell my parents." Pat has taken this one on and saw her taking him to her room today.

Pleased by Year 9 bottom set Classical Studies this morning. They seem a willing group of 14. Year 10 pupil punched Year 8 in corner of eye. After-school detention for him next week but suspect there may be repercussions from Year 8 parents.

For Friday, a quiet day – would we do better to avoid a full assembly on Friday pm? Too rowdy?

The two girls with studs in nose still have them there. Quietly asked to remove by Monday. We shall see; could be building up to a showdown. TGIF[1] offended Dave Gregson, ex-Head of French and now a priest but I understand why it is so often said and I sympathise.

At lunchtime today one Year 7 pupil said, "Do you remember Catherine Noble?" I told her I did and that she had two brothers. I suggested she had left a couple of years ago. "She is my mother."

Tempus does indeed fugit.

[1] *Thank God it's Friday*

Monday 18th September 1995

BY 8.35 am it was a case of 'Weekend? What weekend?' Two calls for me on answerphone. What did we do before them and indeed before nearly everyone had phones? It makes contact, especially complaining and querying so much easier. I shall probably comment on this again when snow or threat of snow occurs.

The calls were about: (1) bad behaviour on buses. Bottles being thrown out of windows at Waterloo; and (2) mother wanting me to contact her regarding her daughter.

This [latter] call was about a disciplinary matter – only I could deal with it. "I only have faith in you, Mr Bush". I tried to explain she should go via the pastoral deputy or year head but could not be dissuaded. I gave way. I shall see her tomorrow at 11.30 am. I'm going to have to solve this one before next year.

11

Incoming call at 8.30 am from parent/governor regarding intimidatory behaviour on the Lepton K.79 [bus]. Pupils are walking as frightened to board bus. Investigation via Year 11 trusties reveal that one notorious Year 8 is the prime mover.

Nicky Green, secretary, reported that the victim of punching last Friday had to go to hospital with blurred vision. 'Accident' report will have to be completed.

Summoned along with Pat by Clive with important pieces of news. Firstly, that a letter from Ofsted[1] had arrived announcing an inspection in Autumn '96 or Spring '97. I tried not to smirk too broadly. Secondly, secretary Ann Watson has resigned and will leave in four weeks' time. Very sad news for me as we have got on so well. It's going to make a tough term tougher in so many ways.

Lunchtime, no break as usual seeing pupils and colleagues. Management meeting 2.00 pm to 4.20 pm. Ran out of time as is often the case but Clive has a plan to spread the LTA[2] referral load. Let's hope it can be made to work. So home by 4.45 pm and the first Adult Spanish Evening Class tonight at 7.00 pm.

A welcome change.

[1]*Office for Standards in Education, Children's Services and Skills, a non-ministerial department of the UK government responsible for inspecting educational institutions*
[2]*Lunchtime Teaching Assistants, a small group of staff engaged to supervise pupils at lunchtime*

Tuesday 19th September 1995

PHEW! It's a pity one unpleasant matter can cast such a dark cloud over the whole day, affecting one's mood and colouring one's judgement. I had two excellent lessons with Year 9 and Year 11 and yet the Lepton bus business dominated the rest of the day.

The complaints of yesterday mushroomed today. The parents who rang yesterday were here promptly at 11.30 am to complain about the Lepton bus. Their daughter had had her nose broken by one of Year 8 pupil's elder sisters. She'll be off for a week or more. The Year 9 [pupil] is clearly terrorising other pupils and a herd instinct or *Lord of the Flies* syndrome has encouraged others to encourage her.

Lunchtime saw a Year 10 pupil showing Clive and me her lower legs, black and blue, dreadful abrasions and real cuts received from her assailant last Friday. The parent, a doctor, had not summoned the police despite the offence being committed on the bus. Not reported directly to us either. Why are such events almost glossed over by some and rigorously pursued by others? This morning's parents have the police involved.

There was a special K.79 assembly where I was grateful that Clive gave me the lead to deliver my Bush's Big Blast and he fully supported. Year 8 excluded for three days – the beginning of the end for her I suspect but then where will she go?

In between all this trying to discuss curriculum plan for '96–'97 with W—— and B——. Little do they know! An hour post school with Simon Russell and Martyn Hicks, and Clive and Bursar trying to placate the Old Almondburian footballers. It's all a matter of style and tact which some have and some don't, I'm afraid.

Wednesday 20th September 1995

AT 8.25 am Year 10 pupil's grandmother arrived with a sad tale of how her granddaughter had been verbally abused by her mother and was rejoining the estranged husband in Harrogate. This happened last year when the girl left for a long time. She's not been back this term. "Will not be returning to KJS". The girl is very upset. She left for Harrogate last Sunday and is to be taken off our roll. At 1.30 pm grandmother rings again. "She is returning to live with me so she can complete her education with us. Will be brought in tomorrow."

And we expect such children to settle down and work hard for their GCSEs[1]. What a dreadful state of affairs.

The life some of these young people lead outside school – their sexual experiences, videos watched, places visited, information about which is picked up, for example, in Home Economics or CDT[2] lessons when they think that the teachers during practicals are completely deaf! All this makes us realise that school must seem very dull to some and 'exciting lessons' in teachers' eyes are very much run-of-the-mill.

More complaints over buses continue to filter through but we seem to be getting on top of that problem for the moment.

Teaching lessons 2 to 4 was a pleasant escape and despite the repetitive nature of the subject matter, the ever-changing nature of the pupils brings new interest and challenges.

Extra management meeting periods 5 to 6 on Wednesdays to be a regular slot. Necessary I suppose, but I find my enthusiasm waning on these occasions and do hope it doesn't show too obviously.

The nose stud saga continues with the Year 9 girl. Pat is now involved. PE department informed me they would not allow her to do PE yesterday. L—— of air gun fame or notoriety *(11th September)* has led to NUT[3] Big Chief being informed and not Clive. Furious as he had involved the police yesterday.

Bus duty and then to curriculum panel 3.20 to 4.40 pm. Passed reasonably quickly but not over enthusiastically. At least I did not feel on the point of nodding off as happened once or twice last year. Poor old V—— looks exhausted and only two and a half weeks gone.

[1]*GCSEs were introduced in 1988 to establish a national qualification for those who decided to leave school at 16, without necessarily pursuing further academic study towards qualifications such as 'A' levels or university degrees. They replaced the former CSE and O-Level qualifications.*

[2]*Craft, Design and Technology, often called woodwork, metalwork and technical drawing prior to 1989*

[3]*National Union of Teachers*

Thursday 21st September 1995

IT's a pity that days are so easily dominated by unpleasant events, recalcitrant pupils, fights and fracas. To retain optimism one has constantly to remind oneself that the majority of our pupils are pleasant, hard-working and keen to learn.

Early part of day saw yesterday's girl brought in by her grandmother. She looked tired and drawn. Let's hope she can settle.

P—— again proving very difficult: his apparently mentally unstable father is to take him again while his separated wife goes off to Portugal with friends for a holiday! He'll have to go to live with his sister if father can't cope. Not surprisingly he's been very difficult today. Clive tries to be sympathetic but tends to accept his story too readily while staff become increasingly frustrated.

Clive produced pages of material regarding attainment grades norm-referenced to be replaced by criteria-referenced grades. I find all this increasingly depressing and irrelevant. I know it has to be – Ofsted will expect it – but it is difficult to relate it immediately to what goes on day after day, lesson after lesson in the classroom. Clive announced receipt of official notice that we shall be visited by Ofsted in 1996. This was in Briefing. 'We' of course does not include me but hardly anybody knows that. Strange feeling.

Afternoon saw planning of tomorrow morning's fire practice. Weather is going to break at weekend so rush to get it all ready for 11.30 am tomorrow. Informed key players for this 'practice practice'.

After school saw more phone calls regarding buses. Another fight. A—— believes we must ride shotgun to stop the surge in bad behaviour which will cost us dearly in bad publicity. Yet sad for poor rivals, Almondbury High School, where two pupils, brothers, have been arrested for the murder of their teacher-mother.

Friday 22nd September 1995

THE recurring problem is how to record all the events of interest at the end of the day, possibly in the late evening, when those events occur so thick and fast during busy days.

The Year 7 pupil already involved in three fights after only three weeks here. The parent ringing up to declare that she was forbidding her child from doing any homework in Home Economics, CDT or Art as these are 'non-academic subjects'. A curse on the telephone. Have I already mentioned that its readiness to hand and its avoiding face-to-face encounters makes it a time-waster, an instrument/weapon for whingeing parents?

Year 11 boy came to report last night's bullying of Year 7 by [Year] 8.

Perhaps the tide is turning. With the cooperation and reporting by older pupils we can crack this bad behaviour on buses.

Had to remove beautifully produced notice by M—— as she had written 'assisstance'. Her spelling is a real handicap. It was she who sent Jack a note at six months advising him of her visit to the anti-natal clinic. "Rather late in the day" we remarked. Earlier I had a note from M——referring to the 'dinning room.' Such a common weakness among teachers these days and bound to become self- perpetuating.

Today's smile came from a little Year 9 girl. "Mr Bush, I've brought 'mi'[1] Classical Studies book. DAB: "No, you mean '*My* book'. Pupil: "I've brought *your* book." DAB: "No – never mind – this conversation could go on and on ad infinitum."

For a Friday a remarkably quiet day. Fire practice went very well. Weather fine. 750 people out in quick time – quiet, good humoured, all present and in again in equally quick time. Spent part of pm MBWA. It's a very effective way of taking the temperature. Local relationships restored when I was able to ring eighty year old to assure him that the wall near Grasscroft will be repaired by L—— from the CDT Dept and Year 11 'volunteers'. He sounded so pleased and relieved. That was a good note on which to finish the week especially as it followed 40 minutes with the Unwind Club in the staffroom. What an excellent sounding board, mine of information and gossip it is.

[1]*Huddersfield vernacular for 'my'*

Monday 25th September 1995

A SPECIAL day in that 'the brightest pupil I have ever taught' spent the day in school. Bryan Hopkinson[1], now British Ambassador in Bosnia, arrived at 8.45 am. He and his charming wife, Stephanie had spent the previous evening with us enjoying a delightful dinner and plenty of jaunts down Nostalgia Avenue. This was resumed during the day as together we pored over the Classics Society minutes from the early '70s and Jack's immaculate Willans Cup records. It's difficult not to feel that standards have dropped or at least that such valuable extra- curricular activities – which are now rare – are not a very sad loss. Bryan spoke to various groups, finding the Year 7s responsive but Year 10s disappointingly reticent.

Clive, Pat and I met to discuss the future, ie management structures after my retirement and that of Jack. It seems Pat is possibly getting cold feet over the thought of only one deputy. From a potentially selfish stand-point – redundancy – and yet a good one for the school, I shall continue to push for one.

Other positive news included P—— taking two Year 11s to repair the dry stone wall in Grasscroft, an excellent job which I saw tonight as I walked home and very good for public relations.

The nose stud saga continues. It's now reached Clive who has explained the school's/governors' rules but I still wonder if [the stud] will be in to-morrow morning when I teach her for periods 1 and 2.

No bus news today although Clive says he took the most abusive phone call ever from a parent – a teacher – whose daughter he had excluded for one day over her violent behaviour. Contrast this with a call from another mother. "Right luv. I've grounded her for a month. She will not do it agin.'

Goodbye to Bryan at 3.30 pm. What a different world he returns to soon.

[1]*King James's Grammar School 1967-74*

Tuesday 26th September 1995

ABIDING impression is of difficulties with Year 11. How pupils change over five years! They enter aged 11 – certainly not innocent and wide-eyed these days – but often cheerful, pleasant and keen to impress. Some remain so, yet in a few cases the po-tential rogue becomes a hard-working salt-of-the-earth young man/woman. More often and sadly, they change quite dramatically to dis-illusioned, switched off and unwilling teenagers.

Two or three shining examples of this today – all girls. But, of course, they are not 'girls'. They are very worldly wise, very experienced young women. Problems have revolved around make up, meeting 'undesirables' at lunchtime, jewellery – the usual. One has to be firm; rules are clearly laid down but lurking sympathies are difficult at times to disguise.

Year 9 nose stud remains, witnessed this morning in Latin periods 3-4. Clive now has a problem as he is determined to make a stand.

I wish he would be more direct in his language sometimes eg "Could we possibly make a little more effort to see if we can manage to be more prompt to lessons?" Instead he might say "Stop short changing the kids and get to your f*****g lessons on time." Not that he would ever say the latter but the sentiment could be conveyed.

Daily dealings with individuals bring heart–rending stories. Year 9 very weak pupil clearly not really wanted by either parent was sent off to relatives in Nottingham at the weekend as there are troubles 'at home'. Aware he could be spinning sympathy – inducing stories – but I feel he is not bright enough. It's a dreadful situation. Classical Studies homework must be a long way down his priority list.

Let's not forget the positive. An excellent Year 11 Latin lesson. Pupils generally very well turned out and cheerful. Constantly reminding myself that this is so important.

Wednesday 27th September 1995

NOT a day to look back on with any great satisfaction. It's so easy to lose track of the real issues amongst the minutiae of every day events.

Nose stud count has risen to 3 today. Three young pupils turned off the K.78 Lepton bus as the driver declared it too full. Having apparently solved the Kirkheaton bus problem, the Lepton buses which previously had problems regarding bad behaviour now replaced by overcrowding. 28 standing last night. Rang the Systems Manager at Yorkshire Rider. "What is the maximum allowed standing?" "Depends on the size of the bus." "How many on the largest single decker?" "I don't know." He doesn't know?! They sent a letter today asking us to investigate a slashed seat on a bus journey of the 14th September i.e. nearly 2 weeks after the alleged offence.

Girl with four earrings in each ear. "Father says I'm not to take them out." Do these things really matter? To the individual they do, I suppose and to the rest of the school at large.

The old gentleman whose wall we repaired yesterday rang movingly to thank us. Half an hour later another phone call from Grasscroft to say someone, probably our pupil or pupils, has been throwing stones at horses there.

I rampaged in assembly of lower school and read an article regarding water difficulties in Sarajevo. Smiling/smirking colleagues told me it had been duplicated and read out at all four house assemblies last Monday. Still R—— was kind enough to say it was still "a rattling good assembly."

Interviewing heads of teams regarding GCSEs results, 38 to 40 minutes each. What a contrast to the days of Harry Taylor, the grammar school head, who dismissed all the results in all subjects in about two minutes in the early 60s.

Pig-in-the-middle when Clive and Pat became heated over attainment grading. This could be embarrassing. Discussed style with Clive and suggested a more direct, tough approach to staff when requesting promptness to lessons. I shall note if there is a change.

The first sentence today is not entirely true as I did enjoy my lessons.

Thursday 28th September 1995

REFLECTING in bed last night on the day's events I realised I had not mentioned another 'first'. A little lad who had to be taken out of my assembly as the sound of hail – which he fears – beating on the flat sports hall roof caused him to tremble uncontrollably, poor chap. As I said yesterday, every individual has his or her own hopes and fears. How difficult to recognise all these in the scurrying activity of day-to-day school life.

And so to Thursday. Nose stud count down to 2. No trouble on buses, as far as I know, but the secretary was taking, as I left, a strongly worded complaint call from somebody in the village. I shall no doubt hear details tomorrow.

Pupil P—— has been excluded. Sad case as explained earlier but he was simply out of control at school. Will not go, stay or do as instructed. He went 'home' to what, I wonder.

Phone call from Allan Dobson, son of Gerald, over the Domesday Book[1]. This is a very expensive gift from a very old Old Almondburian which is no real use to the school. We've had it for some months now and Dobson senior is upset there is no real recognition of his generosity.

19

This typifies the problem of former pupils who don't really comprehend the changing nature of KJS. Its soul may be the same but the body has different clothes and needs different food.

All this was insignificant on a personal level as 'The Letter'[2] arrived today almost 3 months earlier than last year and earlier than expected. Offer of premature retirement to 5 heads and 5 deputies for 31st August, 1996. Sign here to apply. My dilemma is that if there is to be possible redundancy do I apply for early retirement? I have to ring staffing officer, David Barraclough, for guidance tomorrow.

Did two separate PE cover lessons today. Took me back 34 years, when a 23-year-old young, fit teacher was constantly involved in games on a participatory level. Day-to-day happenings included persuading staffroom committee to stand for election again, successfully tracing the author of some obscene drawing and donating three bags of our homegrown apples to the staff. "Must keep t'band in t'nick' as they say in this locality.

More of this theme anon.

[1]*A lavish facsimile of the* Great Domesday Book *purchased by prominent former pupil Gerald Dobson with the intention of presenting it to the school*
[2]*In recent years in each Autumn Term a letter had arrived from Oldgate House offering redundancy terms to a specific number of senior staff*

Friday 29th September 1995

STARTED badly but improved steadily and on reflection, R—— said in the Unwind Club at 4 o'clock, "Not a bad week."

Last Friday I recall we were feeling low, having been bombarded with problems. I know very well that fellow teachers in other schools would regard KJS as paradise compared with the terrible situation they face daily in, for example, inner-city establishments and I have enormous admiration for those who, day in day out, perform so heroically in such energy-sapping and morale-teatimesapping conditions. Nevertheless, it's all relative, as they say.

Clive out until after break. Jack brought problems over registers. Staff absence meant a shortage of register-takers and part-timers declined as they are not paid until 8.45 am. Clive has apparently sorted out this problem, or so he thought, but not to their satisfaction or clarification. I foresaw this and warned him such tightening of the financial belt would be a loss of goodwill and so it's proving at the moment.

Grasscroft resident complained of litter. How dare she? I pick up every morning while locals have dumped builders' rubble and three polythene bags – large – of garden rubbish very visibly.

Had two satisfying lessons despite or because of their diversity. Year 9 bottom set Classical Studies and Year 11 Latin. What excellent students the latter are. Reminded them of SPOES (Society for the Preservation of the English Subjunctive). Adam James and Joanna Blackburn, last year's senior students, were back in assembly for the ceremonial handing over of the Head Boy and Head Girl insignia to the new incumbents. Adam – 'A' in Latin – reports that he is the "Latin scholar" in his English language group at Greenhead College. He relates how embarrassed he feels as his fellow students are taught the basics of English language, even adjectives etc. Adam could explain the finer points in Latin of the imperfect subjunctive in final relative clauses.

Continuing to interview heads of subjects over exam results. I do feel that Clive is just too nice; he needs to question them more directly. He lets them talk too much. But this is just my opinion and probably why I would never make a good Head.

I say again how valuable the Unwind Club is both for the 'members' and for me as I pick up gossip while they unburden themselves and I take the school's temperature.

Rang David Barraclough at Oldgate House[1]. "Fill in the application form; we will discuss the method of 'going' later."

[1] *The offices of Kirklees Education Department*

CHAPTER 2

October 1995

IN HONOREM PATRIS
SPIRITUSQUE SANCTI
HUJUSQE SCHOLÆ SUPERLIN
INARE BLANCHE BROOKE DE
FEENAY RITE POSUIT ANTE
DIEM IV NONAS SEXTILES
ANNO SALUTIS MDCCCLXXXIII

~ Preparations for Open Day ~

Monday 2nd October 1995

FRIDAY should have included a note on a phone call from a Year 7 parent who had informed R—— that she would not send ingredients to make apple crumble in R——'s requested way and, if she insisted, no ingredients would be sent. Mother's method alone would ensure child's participation. I include only to demonstrate how typical of parent power/intervention/stupidity in today's schools.

And so to week five. Nose stud count down to 1. Pat reported very pleasant conversation with the offender's mother who seemed happy to conform.

The day began at 8.10 am when I met on the drive a young man who had alighted from a car having pecked its driver goodbye. Immaculately dressed, yet sporting a Salvador Dali moustache and a pigtail almost down to his backside. 'Art student from Bretton', I concluded and this was immediately confirmed. Three other ITT students arrived in the next 20 minutes. The pigtailed one obviously caused a lot of mirth and nudges in both staff room and classroom. In a comparatively conventional school such as ours it is probably not wise to dress thus and I shall have to point out that he will lessen his chances at interview, no matter how unjust this may seem.

Interviews continued over exam results. A—— and L—— seen. The latter is awkward in that I am involved in the subject's future ie Classical Studies and Latin.

[At] 8.02 am I posted my application form for early retirement. Periods five and six discussing future management roles. It's not going to be easy to change the subject pronoun in 'next year we/you must ensure higher intake in Year 7 because...'

A very busy day – no lunch hour as we had a 15 minute lunchtime discussion with Jack and Pat. 8.15 am – 4.20 pm with no break; eight hours five minutes really non-stop.

Marking brought home for tomorrow morning. Must remember to take photos in as R—— reports that Year 11 girls cannot believe Mr Bush has normal children. I remember as a pupil similar thoughts that teachers have no life outside school.

Apple crumble story number two. Year 7 pupil (not Friday's) brought in some ready-cooked in a tin for today's Home Economics lesson.

Tuesday 3rd October 1995

AS yesterday, no break all day: 8½ hours non-stop and tonight OAS [meeting]. Jack, who starts regularly at 7.30 am, was refereeing a soccer match tonight and then has OAS after. Teachers need their half term break or certainly the majority do. As I have said many times if there were no longer battery-recharging holidays, I'm sure there would be no teaching profession.

Marking by 8.05 am. Briefing and into two enjoyable double Latin lessons.

Nose stud remains in Year 8!

Called in to help out at break in dining room [when] D—— reported A——'s misdemeanours. But she related in her own inimitable, histrionic style in the staffroom before me and textile student with whom I was chatting. "He freaked, he absolutely freaked," she shrieked. Unknown to her the [textile] student's name is Miss Freake! When told afterwards, her typical reaction: "Oh my God, why hasn't she changed her name?"

Had to interview B—— and F—— on exam results on my own; pleased to be independent as Clive investigating M—— slamming hand down on Year 9 boy's wrist. Boy had it bandaged later. Witnesses reported incident to Clive; watch glass shot out in the action. Clive has sought Oldgate House's advice. [M——] is NUT rep and has had previous verbal warning; it looks as if this could be official and local NUT bigwig [brought] in. 20 years ago it would've all been hushed up. When I think back to my own eruptions at times! N—— lifting T—— off his feet with an uppercut etc. How times have changed, how much more civilised we are today!

Afternoon: planning '96–'97 curriculum. How I long to tell them I shall not be part of it. King Midas and the ass's ears!

Long talk over a management issue with Clive and Pat. Pat on bus duty. Grange Moor bus 50 minutes late and how fortunate the first day Yorkshire Rider sent an inspector.

Wednesday 4th October 1995

MATTERS picked up from yesterday included M—— being seen by Clive. He admits hitting desk, probably breaking ruler and damaging watch but denies hitting the boy's hand. 'Victim' still has hand heavily bandaged. No reaction from volatile parents. Could it be that they are plotting against M——? Clive intends seeing the victim again before taking any further action.

Nose stud 2 appeared in the corridor at break. As it passed me, my sharp, loud request saw its immediate removal – ugh – and placed in pocket. Am I in the minority in finding this repulsive?

Year 9 Classical Studies had a purely factual test on gods and goddesses; some did well but for a Set 3 marks were generally very low. These pupils do not know how to learn facts and/or have insufficient willpower to discipline themselves into learning thoroughly. A few big guns will have to be fired before a satisfactory standard is reached. There is little doubt that failure to learn by rote, to soak up facts, simply to memorise is a change – and a deplorable and major one – since the '60s.

Letter from Year 7 parent about buses yet again. She was complaining about her child being left but also about his having to stand on the bus. Tonight inter-bus driver dispute was entertaining but alarming. K.83 was boxed in, blew horn repeatedly and shuffled back-and-forth behind K.79. When finally it got by there was an improper/obscene gesture to the other driver. I phoned *Yorkshire Rider* who were appreciative and promised action.

Lunchtime distressing call from the village shop owned by a Pakistani. Pupils who should not have been offsite anyway, when refused purchase of cigarettes uttered obscene and racist remarks and spat on the door on leaving. G—— was out in her car but no sign of the culprits. Apologies were made to the shopkeeper who, how wisely and how refreshing, laid the blame on the parents and not KJS. I'm contemplating hiding in the shop [in the morning] as the main offender calls there every morning. [At] 2.30 pm met with four Bretton student teachers. They are very impressed by our pupils – how encouraging! But I reminded them of honeymoon period. I really enjoy these seminars and feel that after more than 34 years of teaching I do have so much Nestorian advice and wisdom to pass on.

Curriculum teams after school; an uneventful meeting.

Thursday 5th October 1995

FRUSTRATION before school began or before I got within 150 yards of it. Plans to act undercover to catch yesterday's youngster guilty of racist abuse came to naught as shop was shut and according to neighbouring one remains so until 10.00 am. Later enquiries revealed that pupil visits regularly at night and not in the morning. This will not be allowed to go unpunished.

Nose studs on the increase according to M——— in Year 11 as he asked for guidance during Briefing. Clive under great pressure all day. He forgot about our meeting with B——— to discuss examination results. Most out of character.

Marking for three quarters of an hour this morning – a routine almost therapeutic – yet I do at times find marking a heavy drag. How tempting not to set work which requires long sessions of marking. But I am determined not to slacken my standards on this final lap.

12.30 to 1.55 pm was the most demanding period I have spent so far this term. By 1.55 pm I felt quite drained, not helped by a poor night's sleep. I woke around 4.00 am. School [had] got into bed with me and would not be kicked out!

12.30 pm saw Gerald Dobson's son, Allan arrive. This is all to do with Gerald's really unwanted gift of the £450 Domesday Book and the future of the Taylor Dyson library[1]. Allan is realistic. I began by trying to explain how school life, teachers' commitments, extracurricular activities and pupils' study habits have all changed so much since the grammar school days. Teachers simply do not have the time or energy to do the things they did in the '60s.

Constant stream of pupils to my door, the dining room atmosphere alarming thanks to invasion by Year 8 'undesirables'. Add a visit by the police and Almondbury High School head and deputy. All were adequate proof how busy/hectic life is. This was the lunch break! Took policeman to my Year 8/9 assembly which went well.

27

Afternoon taken up by investigating racist comments and abuse. Apparently all stemmed from a party last year in a 14-year-old's house where there were no parents present. Drink aplenty and paper inscribed 'burn the blacks' set on fire – and then we are expected to pick up the pieces in school when parents have completely abrogated their responsibility.

[1]*A valuable collection of books, mainly about Yorkshire history, formerly owned by King James's Grammar School headmaster Taylor Dyson (1913-1945). The library is now lodged in the care of the University of Huddersfield.*

Friday 6th October 1995

167 DAYS TO GO

FIVE weeks gone. When I mentioned the countdown to Peter Griffin, my very close friend and Vice-Principal at Greenhead College, in the showers after badminton last night, he seemed quite jealous. "That's nearly ⅐ of the year gone", he declared. I think his maths was optimistic but time is beginning to pass quickly. I've noticed before that as routines in teaching become firmly established, the weeks seem to glide by with ever-increasing rapidity.

Not a bad day for a Friday. I did some MBWA during [periods] 7/8 and the atmosphere was generally calm and academic for a Friday afternoon which is always a good time to test the temperature of the school.

Today the weather has been poor with lashing rain during the lunch hour which means not much activity outside. The (fool)hardy few played soccer throughout and came in soaked.

Some surprisingly good results from Year 9 bottom set Classical Studies. However one supposedly brighter member, despite frequent mentionings over the last three weeks, answered to question number one "Name the mountain on which the Greek gods lived": 'Kilimanjaro'.

This was surpassed by a pupil in Year 7 for B—— in Maths. In response to the request to 'write down five even numbers' wrote: 'five even numbers'.

Last night's possible trouble in the village did not materialise and tonight's threatened confrontation may well have been damped off.

Enjoyed this morning's telling of the Apple of Discord story for the nth time. Interviewed F—— and A—— over the French and Maths results.

28

Both very useful and revealing although it's a little embarrassing to criticise A—— too much for comparatively poor results when we work so well together on timetabling and planning.

Had a 20 minute break at lunch – first of the week – singing with just B——. What a delightful interval.

Confiscated rings of Year 11 pupil at lunchtime when she was caught wearing them for the third time. Mother arrived demanding return of same. When returned to her the usual line. "You are picking on her. They are all wearing them". What an exaggerated, annoying, unhelpful response but on reflection an encouraging week

Monday 9th October 1995

166 DAYS TO GO

MONDAY began in earnest with a phone call to the staff room at 8.20 am. "Would you come down to reception to see Mrs M—— ?" A very distressed Mrs M——, whom I have known for over four years, had son and [his friend, both pupils], wearing baseball caps. When removed they revealed two shaven heads. They claimed four 20-year-olds had forcibly held them down at a Saturday night party while their heads were shaved. Police were called in for possible assault but no charges to be pressed. I suspect the boys' story. Mother is ashamed, sick with stress and worry. Poor woman. What a time she is having. Reminded me again of how pupils can change from friendly, cheerful Year 7s to rebellious, surly Year 11s. In five years' time could well have changed again.

Interviewed B—— over Sociology exam results. What a mixed bag she had last year in terms of both students and results. She is doing a PhD on boys' and girls' performance in exams, GCSE in particular –a most interesting study.

Some marking before, at 10.00 am, beginning discussions in Clive's study on future management format and management of day-to-day matters. Apart from lunch break and house assembly this task took the rest of the day ie until 4.15 pm. I found concentration difficult at times. Aging? Boredom? Cold? Another poor night's sleep. Pleased to see the end of the day.

High note, however, was the arrival of *The Annals*[1] beautifully printed on high quality paper by Clive Ainley, Old Almondburian. Excellent propaganda for Wednesday's Open Day.

Disturbing news from Asian shop in the village. More abuse from pupils at 2.30 pm ie truanting. Three Year 10s, [including] almost certainly one who should have been in court today in support of his mother who is seeking an injunction to keep her drunken, wife-beating husband out of the house. This I know is true. Yet son 'not in school' [either].

Tomorrow Clive will investigate.

[1] *A large-format annual account of school life produced in-house between 1987 and 1996. It replaced the school magazine* The Almondburian.

Tuesday 10th October 1995

YESTERDAY'S investigation turned into today's main event although Clive was the one mainly involved. There are so many major decisions pending, so much to discuss about curriculum-planning, tonight's first-of-the-year tone-setting full governors' meeting; yet all his energy and thereby some of ours is taken up by interviewing the three involved in yesterday's and the previous occasion's racist abuse. This aspect was minor when set against the lifestyle led by at least two of the pupils – and by one in particular and his girlfriend. This involves matters, according to him, such as deliberately putting his hand through a glass partition; his father under St Luke's psychiatric hospital care after threatening to murder his mother; visits to houses where drugs are sold; and a girlfriend [being] approached by older men.

These are 14-year-olds all from homes so badly broken. One has already had three surnames since he's been with us. The details are horrific and the school has to pick up the pieces and attempt to teach these in comparatively large classes of comparatively normal children. What is the point of pumping more and more money into education when the background undoes most of what schools are trying to do? It really is a Herculean if not Sisyphean task.

Nevertheless, after a poor Year 9 class which an inspector would have slammed, classes picked up by 11.00 am and when Year 11 finished, I was on a real high. Shall I miss such highs? What will replace them? Holidays in exotic places? More grandchildren? I prefer not to think of all that just yet.

Lunch hour was extremely busy – succession of incidents, interviews and a dash to take Year 10/11 assembly, adrenaline flowing. Shall I dry up one day before I leave? There's always that lurking fear, the actor's nightmare.

Wednesday 11th October 1995

LAST night's first main governors' meeting was uneventful and non-controversial but when Clive met some governors afterwards he was told that they had been informed that Mr Bush was about to submit a request for early retirement. From the subsequent conversation it seems that I shall have to go public in about four weeks' time. Originally I had planned the revelation at Presentation Evening but now it's going to be much earlier still. I am not sure whether I am increasingly anxious or shall be mightily relieved but I feel I am being carried along disconcertingly rapidly by events on matters over which I've no real control. Time for a rethink.

Today was Open Day and tonight is Open Evening so it's been 8.00 am to 9.00 pm today with 1½ hours break at teatime. A mature student who has spent most of the last 10 years in fashion buying/selling, including Harrods, explained how the first few days of teaching had been 'a real eye-opener.' Matters which in business would have seemed so important are now almost embarrassingly insignificant when compared with problems faced daily in schools; and ours is comparatively problem-free.

Our present four [Bretton] student teachers are again very good. I'm sure the quality in approach, if not in academic training, has improved substantially over the last 3½ decades. The Grammar School – 21 staff when I joined and so much praised and revered – contained at least five staff who today would be considered lazy and/or incompetent. Open Day went very well thanks to R—— and glorious weather.

One Year 9 pupil has such psychological problems that he had attempted to embarrass visitors and consequently just cannot be allowed to stay in a normal school situation. The truants/racist abusers are out for a couple of days so peace for some. Pupils or staff?

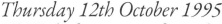

Thursday 12th October 1995

163 DAYS TO GO

AFTER the frenetic pace of yesterday and a generally hectic first 28 days of the term, today was the first time when I properly drew breath. The problem then is, of course, that one feels guilty if every minute is not filled and there is time to reflect on wider issues. This is what management should be about. I have been able to spend more time around the school looking in on classes and helping to defuse acrimonious situations.

Year 11 pupils are generally regarded as our best hope for outstanding results but there is always in Year 11 a minority of disillusioned youngsters who cannot wait to leave. I had a number sent to me at lunchtime by the LTAs. The latter are not trained in handling teenagers, find great difficulty in managing them when they resist or argue. This leads to confrontation which leads to verbal exchanges which leads to Mr Bush. I have to appear to support the adults but have sympathy with the youngsters.

They did find a Year 10 boy banging his head against a tree. He has been repeatedly teased by his peers and despite strong warnings it appears to be continuing. S—— has become involved and stronger action is planned if repeated.

Must remember to ask Clive about the nose stud saga in Year 9 which was at stalemate a week ago. The count seems to be down to one. The standard of dress is generally the highest for some years, perhaps the best ever since the comprehensive era reached King James's.

Another amazing letter from Year 7 parent complaining about the way the PE department attended to an injured finger and signing her name and her nursing qualifications.

Interviewed C—— regarding IS[1] results. Even he admits that the course is glorified Business Studies. Those able pupils whose parents insisted their offsprings' careers depended upon their being on this over-subscribed course are almost wasting their time and should be doing something far more academic.

[1]*Integrated Studies*

Friday 13th October 1995

THE fact that this is being written up at 9.35 pm is in itself significant. If it had been a particularly diary-filling day then it would have been written up on arrival home but for a Friday and the sixth week of term it has been a remarkably smooth and generally very satisfying day. Schools are very much like the English weather; some days dull, cloudy and cool others bright, sunny and rapidly changing too. Today literally and metaphorically sunny despite the date.

Sad to see secretary E—— leave after only 18 months. A delightful person in so many ways yet too tense or intense for school life. Schools do need and require very special kinds of ancillary staff from caretaker to secretary to dinner ladies – they are all so often underrated and always underpaid. E——, for all her responsibilities and skills, earned just around £10,000 per annum.

Taught two very good doubles this morning.

After last night's badminton including one particularly exhilarating game I enjoyed a good night's sleep. Added to this I was less conscious of my hip, now an ache rather than a pain. I felt physically and mentally so much better. Juvenal was so right in his *mens sana in corpore sano*[1]. Teachers need to keep this constantly in mind.

French pupils and teachers were in school today as part of an exchange. I took the two French ladies to lunch, had a post-prandial promenade and showed them and others the school charter and explained its history this afternoon in my fractured French. Retirement could see me really improving my spoken French and Spanish.

At the end of the afternoon I saw a Year 11 girl in my room in tears – a big lass, weak academically and unjustly sent out and to me after being teased by 'pest' boy. She seemed so appreciative of some sympathy and understanding. I bet it's a moment she'll remember but one I shall quickly forget.

[1] *A healthy mind in a healthy body. Juvenal was a Roman poet active in the late first and early second century AD; author of the collection of satirical poems known as the Satires.*

Monday 16th October 1995

MOSTLY an unfulfilling day. It did begin on a positive note with the handing in of Year 11 Latin homework and marking of same. Only one student late for second week in succession. 'Domestic difficulties'. I know the family well. I despair over so many breakups. It does seem comparatively rare these days for any pupil to have a stable family background. All the effort schools put in so readily offset by 'trouble at home'.

Nevertheless, the standard achieved by Year 11s in their first GCSE comprehension exercise was outstanding in many cases. They really are a superb set with which to finish my career and I do hope their results next August justify my optimism.

Lady from Grasscroft came in with a bag of litter collected after pupils came in this morning. When I came down [Grasscroft] it was more or less immaculate. So all between 8.10 am and 8.35 am. Infuriating! She was pleasant, understanding and, like me, frustrated. Apparently she does it most days and there was I innocently believing things had improved.

Supervised/covered a lesson for H—— bottom set Science. How ill disciplined they are. So easy to label a year as weak and thereby the self- fulfilling prophecy syndrome occurs. Yet these really are very poor and as H—— says "1999 results? Just wait!" General opinion is that the other half year is worse.

It has always amazed me how years vary one from another. With around 200 pupils in any one year things should average themselves out But they don't. Why? What forces are at work which give each year its own characteristics? There's a Ph.D in there for someone unless it's already been done.

Lunchtime saw a succession of problems brought by the LTAs. Rudeness and foul language seem to be the norm. Language which older generations find disgusting is commonplace among pupils. Two or three very unpleasant incidents to follow up tomorrow.

Clive running out of patience with pupil N—— who is now mainly on the loose and really is not fit for a school situation.

Management 5/6 discussing general matters prior to a full staff meeting. The staff were remarkably docile and there was no controversy but also little contribution. S—— nodding off; he looks drained. Even perky C—— declared herself "losing patience. We need a break." I agreed. As I've said previously if there were no regular breaks there would be no teaching profession.

A Year 7 pupil who brought in only a banana to make yoghurt told the teacher that his mother said the school would provide the yoghurt.

Tuesday 17th October 1995

GENERALLY a better day but did not begin particularly well. I pointed out that as the deputy had been appointed to the headship at Almondbury High School H—— might well apply for the vacancy. This would mean one of our greatest assets going to our greatest rival and [it] would scupper the plans for the reorganisation of our management team. I may have to play my joker early and reveal to H—— my plans and our intentions.

Went to Year 9 Latin to give a test which I had badly prepared; a test on which they performed poorly for the most part. Quick thinking led to my not collecting in the marks and some rapid morale- boosting exercises. They do need cosseting and, of course, I am always conscious of the need to have a viable group next year, not as though....

It's at times like these that I have sometimes wished I taught Maths, for example, because this would mean the removal of the worry of forming a viable group and I could have taught a 'valuable and essential' subject with more freedom. Still, too late to retrain now.

Year 11 Latin excellent as always.

I received a call at 12.00 noon to say that two Year 10s had been seen down Somerset Road. One only 90% certain over identification. The computer list tells me he should be in N——'s class and I visited the same. "Do you have D—— in your class? "Not sure so I'll have a look at the list". This is after 6½ weeks with a small group, two hours 10 minutes per week. "Is he here?" An embarrassed half smile for he had no idea and no register had been taken. This is a person nearing retirement. Murray White, HM Inspector, once said "It would greatly improve the quality of the teaching profession if we paid 3% to stay at home."

Year 7 Harvest Festival meant a pleasant break from the norm in assembly. How will they be in five years' time?

Planning a revised school day and Ofsted primary information with J—— and C——. How I long to be able to tell them regarding next year.

Pupil A—— was in after-school detention. This is the one with the third surname since he has been with us. Yesterday the father, or rather stepfather, was convicted of drunken-driving and also issued with an injunction which means he has to be out of the house by the end of the month; and if he raises his fist or voice the police are to be informed. I detail this only to ask how we can expect normal behaviour from this pupil when he's in school.

Wednesday 18th October 1995

A VERY busy day. At times that feeling of being overwhelmed. Even if I tried, it's impossible, I'm sure, to record a day such as today. For there were many moments when I was being called to the phone at break; while being asked for at the staffroom door; while in discussion with B—— over a problem pupil in Year 9; while... I suppose walking round with a tape recorder might work but I would feel rather pretentious and self-conscious.

A fax arrived this morning which we should have framed. A pupil had been put in after-school detention on Tuesday but because of various misunderstandings she had missed her bus and had to walk home in the rain. This resulted in nearly two pages of dreadful abuse with threats from the parent who is known to be volatile. Should we ignore or apologise? It was clearly the school's fault but hardly worthy of such a tirade.

Year 8 Latin was a pleasure today. It's gratifying to have a class well organised, well disciplined and then to be able to relax and share humour. I delight in seeing them coming alive, warming to one's style. I discussed this with our four Bretton student teachers this afternoon. I repeat how much I enjoy these seminars and how much I feel I have to give. Will all this come to an end and so suddenly? Would I have the same immediacy and impact if I were not actually at the chalkface? It's again very satisfying that they seem so appreciative and interested.

Another hour with Clive and Pat this morning discussing future management structures. Nearly all Clive's work but a plan seems at last to be emerging. Tomorrow could be very significant. A lot of money could rest on that meeting! I'll try to subjugate personal financial interest to the Greater Good of KJS.

Nose studs count: two today. Year 9 Little Miss Defiant brought set of books to my room. In my old-fashioned way I find it difficult to be civil when my eyes are drawn to a small piece of metal. Spotted another while on bus duty. Annoyed on a personal level as it's someone I have helped a lot.

Thursday 19th October 01995

TIME 9.40 pm! 2½ hours badminton tonight brought a feeling of physical exhaustion after mental exhaustion by 4.30 pm. Nevertheless, it is still remarkable how vigorous exercise can restore one's drained mental state.

Today was one of the most demanding so far this term, dominated by three events: an irate phone call at 8.35 am, N—— visiting from Oldgate House and an off- the-rails Year 10 [pupil].

The phone call was from a lady who had been spat at by a pupil on the bus coming up Almondbury Bank who then waved provocatively at her. She was livid and rightly so. We have a good description but despite 30 minutes devoted to this have no success so far. Tomorrow all K.83 blonde boys will stay behind. Unfortunately the lady turns out to be a teacher at a local rival [school], Almondbury High School.

9.15 am: Three students from the University of Huddersfield arrived (ITT). Two should be OK but immediate worries over a 40-year-old plus, slow speaking Asian whom I found difficult to understand. I cannot imagine him in front of a class of some of our Year 10 non-racially sympathetic pupils but there have been surprises before.

N—— was here to discuss management structures for next year and this lasted for one hour. She seems happy with the proposed arrangement but alarm bells sounded at the end when she heard I had applied to retire under the premature retirement scheme. She suggested this might preclude redundancy. I explained that David Barraclough had assured me it did not and I have to have faith in his advice.

A 30 minute lesson with Year 8 Latin was an improvement but generally this year is very ill disciplined. Huge pile of marking this week, badly timed. I should have spread it more.

The truant of Tuesday was late yet again this morning. B—— and I saw his parents at 3.15 pm for 40 minutes. What an alarming situation. From a well balanced pupil he has become a rebellious, defiant 14-year-old who regularly gets drunk on the recreation ground near where we live, is a dreadful liar and skips lessons regularly. Some very straight talking and lesson by lesson report. Will we manage to save him?

High notes at the end of the day when two parents visited us with a view to sending their 11-year-olds to KJS. They have been delighted with the place.

Also, as I walked home, I called in to watch part of a football match with our Under 15s beating Almondbury High 6-1 and it was only half time.

Friday 20th October 1995

THE end of the first half term. One sixth of the academic year but more in actual days. As daughter said on the phone two minutes ago, "Dad, you shouldn't wish your time away." I'm not really doing so but it's fascinating noting the balance between 'gone' and 'to go '.

If anyone had managed to enter my room between 7.55 am and 8.20 am I should probably have been given early retirement on breakdown grounds. Having been soaked to the skin from thighs down while walking to school in a downpour, I sat in the dark in my room sporting my very loud boxer shorts (a present from grandson Jordi), while my trousers dried on the radiator. My door was locked and I marked in the gloom. Numerous knocks and attempts to open the door to bring in homework.

2½ hours badminton last night meant a good night's sleep and in turn led to two very satisfying lessons between 8.45 and 11.00 am. This was especially so because I launched into Virgil's *Aeneid Book 12*, his last book, the last lines, and for my last time. How appropriate.

Highly alarming reports over the maths student [teacher] mentioned yesterday. He was late and told the second in maths he preferred his lessons as the Head of Department's were old-fashioned. I can hardly understand him and the pupils have no chance. Rang Professor Newbold at University of Huddersfield to say "Help! Don't send him in again.We have a real problem here with possible racist implications".

Assembly saw the grand lottery/raffle draw: £2400 raised, with Jonathan Dyson[1], former Head Boy and Huddersfield Town football star, making the presentation. It all went very well except that the *Huddersfield Examiner* photographer did not turn up and did not let us know.

Kept K.83 pupils back to try to discover the 'spitter'. Dismissed all girls, all dark haired boys and all non-Kirkheaton bus travellers. I got down to the last 15. Yet the guilty party had slipped out by lying about the bus he caught that morning. However, he was shopped by five or six 'grassers'. When interviewed, he denied it all. I have never seen Clive so loud and direct with a pupil. Is he beginning to assume my role? The boy's father has already been in jail for going into a school and assaulting pupils. Boy is petrified, I suspect. To be continued post half term. The boy is already in trouble for head-butting.

The truant of yesterday was late again this morning by only a few minutes. Clive is talking of expelling pupil B—— who is in trouble yet again.

Incredible interview between Head of Year H—— and Year 7 parent at 8.20 am. A long list of complaints all of which were unfounded and mother completely misled by her daughter. Felt very sorry for Head of Year who has to ring the complaining mother tonight.

Twenty minutes of constant laughs in the Unwind Club after school. Great relief and very much needed. Clive and Pat both joined in.

[1]*Jonathan Dyson (King James's School 1985-90) made over 200 appearances for Huddersfield Town from 1991-2003.*

HALF-TERM BREAK

Monday 30th October 1995

PHEW! ...for a number of reasons, so much so that a small brandy was called for around 5.00 pm in the hope that it would release some tension. 5.30 pm and it has not yet worked. Part of the reason for that familiar, ache-under-the-ribs and shortage of breath is, no doubt, the contrast between last week's stay with daughter, husband and grandson Jordi in Porthcawl and the immediate pressures by 8.20 am this morning.

Worse for Clive in that he had little apparent relaxation last week and he came up to my room at 8.30 am to report the alleged spitter's father was in reception. The latter has already been in jail for entering another school and for violent conduct therein. We were to be on call. Not needed although the father protested son's innocence. The latter had not told him he had already confessed to spitting if not at a pedestrian. It'll be a couple of days before we have time to follow this up.

Piles of marking building up which is somewhat depressing but was offset when I began to award very high marks to Year 11 Latin on their first GCSE paper. Contrast this with Year 9 Classical Studies set three of six whose English, spelling and punctuation is terribly weak. Back to some basics. How can such comparatively intelligent pupils have reached this stage ie age 14 – and still make such elementary errors?

Spirits lifted again when Professor Newbold rang from the University of Huddersfield to say that W—— (Maths student [teacher]) had 'done a bunk'. It seems he was often drunk and a problem to fellow students and security staff. What a relief, presuming he will not return.

11.30 am to 12.30 pm spent with Clive and Pat discussing the budget, future management structure and in particular how and when I shall reveal my retirement plans. It was during this time that I felt very ill at ease and apprehensive. I shall be greatly relieved when the news is public.

Lunch was hurried as so much marking to do and felt guilty about missing house assembly.

Management meeting delayed when Clive and Pat met with the problem D—— twins. Priorities. The interest of the individual versus the general interest of the school is a constant problem. At the end of the day I felt that I had seen very little of my colleagues, which I regret as I see this as a very important part of my role.

Tuesday 31st October 1995

A COMPARATIVELY quiet beginning to the day. Year 11 Latin followed by Year 9 Latin is a privileged way to begin a teacher's day. However, I do teach such classes very intensively so that I find after 2½ hours I am feeling quite drained.

Spent the first 15 minutes of break giving extra tuition to two Year 11 pupils, one of whom is very able but seems again to be having psychological problems. I wonder if the problem lies with the parents, but no proof. So often the fault does lie with the adults and not with the child.

Little Miss Nose Stud in Latin lesson. Clive will see her again but reluctant to press the issue as he is sure the LEA would not ultimately support an exclusion.

The day, I remember, had begun with three Year 11 trusties reporting major incident on the K.83 last night. An Indian driver plus provocative behaviour by our pupils led to an exchange of racist comments and much swearing. The driver manhandled a Year 10 pupil who in turn hit the driver in the face. Both apologized to each other at the end of the journey. Emergency doors opened. Spent one hour over this during and after lunch – to be continued/concluded tomorrow. How much time and energy have been involved with buses so far this term! One has to compromise and allocate blame in a fairly arbitrary manner. There seems a possibility that the Kirkheaton buses may be leaving from the bus bay at the school and not from the village. This would help.

Timetable discussion this afternoon with C—— and L——. I was on the point of telling them about premature retirement but bit my tongue. I am trying to pass more and more onto them. I wonder if they have guessed.

Father of spitter in school again. He has banned his son from using the bus but still no admission of guilt.

Two incidents to indicate pressures under which children come to school these days. Pupil A had taken an overdose as he was moved from one step parent to another. Pupils B & C, sisters, two weeks in care after their father threatened to murder the mother, are now back with the estranged father – and come to school and normality?

CHAPTER 3

November
1995

~ Founders' Day ~

Wednesday 1st November 1995

THE 8.30 am phone call as usual meant parent-with-problem or parent-on-rampage demanding my attention. It turned out to be a Year 7 child's parent and I was relieved to pass it on to the Head of Year. The problem is that I am seen by so many as the General Problem Solver and I must wean such people off me and onto the relevant channel before next September.

Discussed with G—— possible solutions to the IT coordinator post when B—— goes at the end of the year. There are complaints from his Year 10 class. This is a man who has basically struggled for much of his time with us. I wonder if he would be allowed to continue teaching under a new regime?

After a very good Year 8 Latin lesson my double Year 9 Classical Studies was very poor. Timing was completely out, the atmosphere far from conducive and delivery not smooth and that's after 34 years of teaching. The main problem is they really are poorly disciplined in an organisational sense and it's taking a long time – too long – to get them accustomed to my methods. Should I be more flexible? No break as seeing 4/5 of them over their work.

11.30 am to 12.30 pm in discussion with Pat and Clive regarding the curriculum '96/'97 and a radically restructure for '97/'98. This will be when I shall be far away, already forgetting about KJS ...or shall I?

Hurried lunch and back in 10 minutes to continue investigation into yesterday's bus business. So many involved I cannot exclude all so arbitrarily I have to decide on the four worst offenders in the hope that they will 'encourager les autres'. 'Sentence' tomorrow.

Adrenaline fast flowing and off to Key Stage 3 assembly. It went well, I felt. 'Honesty' theme. 450 pupils in absolute silence and in the palm of my hand. A feeling of power yet great, fragile responsibility. From this to a Nobody in September '96?

Enjoyed another 40 minutes with ITT students but one is not well and struggling badly this week. He needs help.

Bus duty as the fading autumn sunshine lit up the yellowing trees in the Farnley Valley, a really beautiful scene.

Singing for 30 minutes with M—— and O—— including a Spanish Christmas Carol.

Term must be racing on!

Thursday 2nd November 1995

153
DAYS TO GO

BRIEFING this morning was, as often, very revealing. Most annoying that R—— had told an ITT student [teacher] he had no need to attend. If he had, he would have heard about pupil S—— in Year 10, difficult but quite bright, whose parents are separating and whose grandmother is dying from a brain tumour. No wonder he is less balanced than in Year 7. 'A dog is for life, not just for Christmas'. What a comment on our society's priorities. How about 'A child is for life not just for a few years of marriage'? S—— had paid £10 to another pupil on Monday for breaking his watch. Yesterday, hammering on a window, he broke it so another bill for £10.

A Year 7 boy has a phobia over rain. Did I record he had had to leave an assembly in a distressed state when it hailed on the flat roof? Apparently he fears all rain – fear of being carried off in a flood – even black clouds cause him acute anxiety. "All staff to be sympathetic."

Clive recounted to me his annoyance with three of this year's Year 10 tutors who had avoided any serious attempt to bring parents into last night's tutors' meeting. They had left within the first 45 minutes. "No customers". We'll see if Clive is able to tell them off effectively.

A glorious autumn morning as I accompanied Mr Bloxholme, school buses supremo, out into Big Tree Yard to discuss bringing the Kirkheaton buses down to the bus bay. Two weeks on Monday if all goes well. There will be problems but the advantages strongly outweigh the disadvantages; we must make it work. Some extra work for staff but I shall have to convince them that it is for the General Good.

For the first time in a while, I was able to do some MBWA this afternoon. Very rewarding as always and, I believe, reassuring to colleagues. Year 11 boy whose parents declare that KJS is "pathetic – it suspends for nothing" [is] back from suspension. Today he admitted to spitting in Year 10 girl's hair. Note sent to parents and phone call requested.

NB: 90% of pupils pleasant and well-behaved. I must constantly remind myself of this.

Friday 3rd November 1995

ANOTHER Friday! Eight weeks of the year over already and one more person knows of my intentions. Clive asked that I let our Bursar know as forward planning meant increasing difficulties if she remained in ignorance. She did express regret but interestingly also revealed that 'others' – as vague as that – did periodically query with her the possibility of my leaving.

Day began at 8.25 am with 'emergency meeting' called by Clive and Pat. Bus [problem]: K.83 driver so incensed by pupils' behaviour that last night he brought the bus back to the bus bay. Trusties revealed that the driver had initiated trouble by inappropriate, foolish remarks to a partially sighted pupil. He said: "You look as if you've just woken up!"

Year 9 Classical Studies reminded me yet again how pleasant yet how very weak the lowest ability pupils can be. But one did raise the smile of the week. "The Greeks slipped out of the horse's b——. Complete the word." "Bum" was the first word offered. Another improved with "bottom" before one eventually suggested "belly" which they had been given last week.

Interview with the Performing Arts team over large PE classes. I know it's a very sexist comment but PE female teachers do seem of a type. 'Defensively aggressive' if that's not too oxymoronic.

Enjoyed a 20 minute sing with just R—— at lunchtime, the first escape during the lunch hour as usual this week. Tucked away in a music practice room I still felt somewhat guilty. It's like trying to relax after intense work.

In assembly Clive spoke about his Tanzanian guest, all very interesting but I sensed it went on far too long.

The week finished on a disturbing, discouraging and disconcerting note. The bus duty team reported bad behaviour in the yard. Poor queueing etc and then the Unwind Club for 40 minutes deplored the state of discipline in the school. They said they were afraid to speak up at staff meetings as they believe Clive takes it as a personal insult.

Spent until 4.40 pm talking to Clive and Pat regarding some of the above points but didn't want to spoil their weekend by seeming too blunt.

They had mentioned in the staffroom the problem of smoking among pupils. How appropriate that a parent should ring up to complain, politely but forcibly, that her daughter's pullover had been burnt by a thrown, lit cigarette.

Monday 6th November 1995

THAT Monday morning feeling! Doubly depressing in that I had not done much school work over a pleasant, mostly sunny weekend and therefore ought to have been feeling refreshed and secondly because I have not felt this way so far this term. Why? There seemed, so I reflected as I walked to school, so many matters to deal with in the immediate future. Minor disciplinary ones to Founders' Day service, OAS Dinner and speech, bus reorganisation and staff reaction, last Friday's general moan etc. What will life be like this time next year on a day-to-day basis? Will I be bored when life is, I presume, much simplified?

By 8.30 am I was discussing the burnt pullover affair from Friday afternoon – really very minor although the problem of smoking on buses is widespread and hardly new. Confine 50, 60, 70 youngsters in a small space at the end of the day and there are bound to be problems. Historically more for us for, as previously explained, most of our pupils come to school by bus.

By 10.00 am we were discussing 'future management structures' again and from then until 3.40 pm, with a lunchtime break, we were in meetings. Clive, so hard-working, had spent nearly all Sunday preparing his impressive document. Convincing although I wonder if the governors will really understand it or fully appreciate it. Would most be happy to let the manager manage?

At 10.00 am two year 11 girls brought a particularly offensive document about themselves written by two others. I had to appear sympathetic but they have by their own conduct invited it. Such hatred – a word used advisedly – is upsetting and neither party wishes to compromise or make peace.

Invited to a pastoral meeting after school where there was to be a letting off of steam and representing of staff concern. There is a clear division between the "hit 'em hard, including staff" brigade and the "gently, gently, let's find out the reason" camp.

To be continued.

 ## Tuesday 7th November 1995

A BRANDY in my coffee, quite a large one – partly medicinal, partly celebratory – was called for on returning home this evening. At 2.30 pm I had THE phone call which, I suppose was instrumental in instigating the next stage of my life.

It came in the middle of a regular weekly meeting with S—— and W—— regarding timetabling and forward planning. It was [a telephone call] from Oldgate House, Kirklees Education Headquarters. Suspicious and suspecting it was of some import I excused myself from my own room and took it in L——'s office . It was from Helen Moriarty, informing me that Kirklees were making me an offer for premature retirement.

I was emotionally stunned; I had anticipated it but its significant finality affected me deeply. I did not ask her what the offer was but I presume it is on the original terms. I thanked her for her promptness in letting me know and I stood in silence for some 2 to 3 minutes. Then I made the decision that I could not return to S—— and W—— and continue in a matter-of-fact way. I told them of my intentions. They too looked stunned but offered me their very best wishes and said many kind words. There was no point in telling S—— and not his wife so I visited her as I knew she was free. She was very emotional and so was I. She insisted on coming back to my room with me. I shall most probably spend half an hour with them later tonight when S—— returns from a governors' finance subcommittee meeting.

The rest of the day's events are naturally of minor interest. Nevertheless, I should record that I feel I taught two cracking Latin lessons. How satisfying to say that in the twilight of one's career!

Launched the new bus scheme in Briefing and, I trust, in a half hour lunchtime meeting convinced the Duty Team Leaders that we've got to make this work.

I'm happy but not in a demob sense.

Wednesday 8th November 1995

A VERY mixed day. *Nytol* had meant a solid night's sleep after yesterday's excitement and, despite the expected groggy first hour, I felt the benefit by the time the day was getting under way.

The C——'s popped into my tray a card. "Much loved, C—— and D——.' How kind and how moving. I think I shall have to have a file to put all my letters and cards in, I write immodestly; I'm sure there will be some. Clearly my going will provide opportunities for promotion but I must be aware of any charges of a Machiavellian approach. Everything must be done in the school's interests.

I had a very good lesson with Year 8. One knows when the lesson is going well and even in the 36th year of teaching it still provides a real buzz. How convinced I am of the value of such Latin lessons as they contribute so much in a wider context to language learning and comparative philology and cultures.

In Classical Studies it is a real battle this year as I try to accustom them to my ways and standards. Today, however, did provide the smile of the day. Pupil R——, who was difficult to very difficult in Years 7 and 8 and could never be persuaded not to call out, is at last being coached into putting his hand up. I noticed the raised hand and asked, "Yes, R——?" A pause followed by a genuine, embarrassed grin. "I forgot to put my hand down, sir".

Periods five and six with Pat and Clive for an extra management meeting. As Pat pointed out we are now meeting for up to 8 lessons per week formally and more informally. Yet with £X million pounds of plant, 750 pupils, 42 teaching staff and so many auxiliaries and a budget of £1 million we do need the time. However, disproportionately so much of it taken up by awkward parents and a minority of badly behaved children.

At lunchtime up to 15 pupils set about one of last year's leavers who had come to help with Spanish conversation. The herd insect instinct yet again and shades of *Lord of the Flies*. I was disgusted, infuriated and very much embarrassed that this should happen at KJS. Heads will roll as our investigation continues.

Time spent with the ITT students was enjoyable as ever. Curriculum

Panel and debriefing of same to Clive. Nearly 9 hours without a break. Some will no doubt do more than this but it is really a very intensive way of life!

Thursday 9th November 1995

A STRANGE mixture of a day with a number of highs and lows as often the case. The continued investigation into yesterday's lunchtime incident took up much time and nervous energy and, of course, there comes a point when one has to say 'enough'. Blame is apportioned as accurately and fairly as possible within the time constraints and one hopes the pupils accept this. Clive will do the excluding tomorrow. I should like to believe that most of the offenders are genuinely sorry on reflection.

Why is it that identically planned lessons with supposedly identical forms never work out the same, especially in the timing? This mystified me last year, I remember. An articulate pupil, put on the Bridge[1] by S——, dropped into the conversation that the latter has Parkinson's disease[2]. "I know this because my uncle has it at the age of 48" This is the first time I have heard a pupil say this. How does one deal with it? It continues to put Clive in a difficult situation.

Jonathan Dyson, former KJS Head Boy and Huddersfield Town footballer mentioned two weeks ago, was up again for photos and autographs. He remains such a delightful a person as ever but it's still very much "Yes, Mr Bush. No, Sir." Some fifth or sixth form leavers, on the first evening for example at badminton, cannot wait to get in their 'Daves'.

A Year 11 pupil was sent to isolation for saying "You can't do anything in this f****** school. "When challenged, he exclaimed "Sir, I didn't say it, I swear, I swear." "Yes, that's why you're here." I was quite proud of my witticism but guess it was not appreciated by the offender.

Again I managed to get around a number of classes. It's very gratifying to be told by staff how much they appreciated it and the pupils too. In a Year 8 geography class where they were studying weather, I told them that my mother-in-law says "If you do not like the English weather wait a minute. What does she mean by this?" A small girl on the front row

50

replied, "She means it is so unpredictable that..." What an answer and what a thrill!

Went to Year11 assembly [with] adrenalin gushing, especially after yesterday. I felt that they listened well and accepted my reflections on yesterday and thoughts on honesty and neighbourliness. Or did they? I shall never know. One just lives in hope and faith that some things are taken in.
[1] *The 'bridge' linked the area outside the staffroom (formerly D3 and D2) to the new teaching block. It was used as an area for detaining miscreants.*
[2] *The teacher did have Parkinson's disease and later sadly died*

Friday 10th November 1995

FRIDAY EVENING. After a superb lamb *a la Navarra* dinner and Australian red wine, crossword and log fire – and rain at last in drought- stricken Huddersfield and Halifax – I could be seeing today, and indeed the week, from a somewhat comfortable, gourmet standpoint. Indeed the threatened water cuts and threat to the Old Almondburians' Dinner two weeks tomorrow night are taking up considerable time and causing much anxiety. Bursar, happy to don her prophetess of doom garb, is in her element, predicting dire consequences. Yet the position is very serious.

Nevertheless, putting that worry to one side it has been generally a very satisfying albeit tiring day. The Wednesday afternoon incident was finally dealt with. One girl added to exclusion list who admitted to flicking her lit cigarette onto the victim's arm. All seem to accept their punishment except one who argued, thereby receiving the very sharp end of Clive's tongue. Is he changing, anticipating the necessity to take on at least part of another's mantle?

Year 9 Classical Studies was very satisfying yet Year 11 Latin for the first time was not so. Entirely my fault as I had prepared/duplicated insufficiently for the next section and so ran out of material 10 minutes before the end. Annoying and frustrating as time is so precious with this group.

Lunchtime: Clive left the premises by 1.00 pm so felt guilty having 10 minutes sing with L—— in preparation for the end of term concert and carol service. The main event of the day to which I had to build up was the Remembrance Service. For the last time, I was to read the names of the 35 Old Almondburians who died in the last World War. This time I led the service and introduced it by talking of my own very moving visit to Ypres, Verdun and the First World War cemeteries. I also mentioned my mother, 90 tomorrow and her losing her brother in the RAF. The pupils were excellent – not a sound. At the end, prayers over, heads were raised yet still silence. I slowly fastened on my watch which had been removed to time the one minute silence and Pat and I left in absolute silence. Still very tense and I could have drained a brandy. No wonder actors take to the bottle at the end of performance.

Visited nearly every classroom during periods seven and eight. L——said "Transformation since last week". Why? Went out to the buses in the pouring rain. 15 minutes late. 'Kingfisher' is now emblazoned on the side of the buses. Rang the bus company to protest at the lateness and felt like mentioning Halcyon Days. Hardly! But quite sure the classical reference would not have been appreciated.

Monday 13th November 1995

SCHOOLS are affected by weather – little doubt about that. It's a commonly held belief that wind causes children to be high while constant rain means that they are inside at break and lunch. With no chance to let off steam this causes restlessness. Snow brings alarm, panicking parents and school closures but this is the first time in 35 years that drought has led to hours of contingency planning. Huddersfield and Halifax nationally the only places to be in such a critical state that by a week today rota cuts, emergency tanks etc are all planned. One hour discussing this this morning then at 4.00 pm announcement that all is to be delayed until the end of the month. Let's hope it pours before then because the consequences would be very, very difficult. Another worry for management!

Covering period 2 for G—— who was off for the last three days of last week but was seen shopping in Sainsbury's with his wife and children. Off again today. Colleagues not very pleased. How does Clive deal with such unwise action especially when we suspect the cause of his absence goes deeper ie avoiding the classroom?

Discussion with Pat/Clive about tomorrow night's meeting with the governors' staffing subcommittee.

Important developments over the weekend, as on Saturday morning I received written confirmation of 'the offer' and a booklet on 'pensions'. On Sunday night, I completed my acceptance and also bank details for the payment of a lump sum. This, I noted, would have been on 1st September but as this is a Sunday it will be on 2nd September – quite a nice birthday present!

Quick lunch and then worked our way through a list of problem children. Full assembly today, instead of house assembly, to practise for a week today when all buses will be leaving from the bus bay. Some 500 to 600 pupils to line up in Big Tree Yard and to dismiss from the same. Actually went very well and pupils were very well-behaved.

Management 7 and 8 but Pat was called out to a very disturbing case of child abuse. Don't think I/we were aware of this term 'child abuse' in 1961. Sign of the times? Progress or depressing?

The news I mentioned earlier about the delay in water restrictions removed worries over the OAS dinner a week on Saturday. Great relief for the chairman, DAB.

Tuesday 14th November 1995

CLIVE having car problems this morning so I stepped into the Briefing breach at 8.25 am. Singularly simple this morning with little of the type of information which is so useful for our ITT [teacher training] students. One or two domestic problems but they are so run-of-the-mill that they seem hardly worth recording. As each week, Year 9 and 11 Latin are still a delight. To see the awakening of an interest in etymology in 14-year-olds is still very gratifying. Clive and I discussed this at 4.00 pm tonight. Rather movingly, he said that he and his wife, Irene were discussing my departure and had wondered what he would most miss. He mentioned in particular our exchange of classical clips/references and our ruminating on the origins of words and expressions. With Mike Thornton's death last April one fewer to fly that particular flag. Sadly it's difficult to see the same type of person among our younger staff. They are gifted in other ways but I do feel, as does Clive, that modern education does not breed that type of academic which was the norm when I began teaching in the 60s. There is R——, of course, but he is over 50.

The bottles of drinking water arrived today for distribution when the drought rota cuts begin. Hundreds if not thousands of them. Storage is a real problem. C——'s form had to act as carriers to help bring them in as they were not on pallets.

Jack and I were called to patrol outside as visitors/undesirables were on the premises. What will they do when we've both gone? Who will fill our authoritarian shoes? Or is this yet more hubris? Shall I really want to know from Chepstow or Devon or wherever we settle?

Meeting with W—— and B—— to discuss curriculum '96/'97 I do find it difficult, now that they know, to say 'you' and not 'we'.

Spent 20 minutes in the office post 4.00 pm yarning with L—— and Jack, both good raconteurs with real wit. How I shall miss them!

Tonight is the governors' staff subcommittee at 8.00 pm. More people will be taken into confidence. Redundancy of many thousand of pounds could depend on this. Deep breath.

Wednesday 15th November 1995

THE fact that I was not home until 10.20 pm, mind a-racing, awoken by alarm at 6.50 am and into school again by 8.00 am meant that I was somewhat edgy initially this morning. An important visitor at 9.00 am. Last night's protracted meeting did not reach a decision ie no recommendation yet to full governing body on 14th December. The chairman apparently has some procedural misgivings but there was a clear majority in favour of the New Plan. They, understandably perhaps, want more time to reflect and there is a second meeting planned for two weeks' time. Fingers crossed.

9.00 am saw the arrival of Tony Chisholm from Bretton Training College plus four students and four teacher tutors. I do enjoy so much this aspect of my work but I had little time to talk as I was teaching periods 2, 3 and 4. The student he saw is struggling. Sad, for he is a conscientious young fellow. His lesson was a 'failure' and Tony will be back to see him again in three weeks' time. What is it that gives a teacher ease of control? Factor 'X' I've always termed it; very difficult to define and even more difficult to inculcate. The most unlikely ones often have it while others, outwardly promising, don't.

Discussed last night's meeting with Clive and Pat for an hour. At 1.35 pm I realised I was to take a Year 10 assembly at 1.40 pm! 20 years ago I would have been seized by panic. A quiet gulp, books gathered, a theme thought up on the way and Year 10 in the palm of my hand. Thanks be to God for experience, as I explained to the ITT students at 2.30 pm. Very annoyed, however, that only two Year 10 tutors present in that assembly. Do I say anything or opt for the quiet life and exit? I may be taking Briefing in the morning and I may be very tempted to say something.

Languages Department meeting until 4.30 pm. The proposed changes to the school day for September '96 are going to have union opposition as they involve a longer day. We are below the norm. What a pity there is no standard day/week.

Thursday 16th November 1995

TEMPUS celerrime fugit[1]. 25% of the year already gone. 3.30 am saw me downstairs having a Lemsip, paracetamol etc; bad throat, headache and the like. Should have had the day off but didn't, of course, for DAB is never off. Stubborn pride forbids. Only five days off in my 34+ years. A proud boast and I desperately hope there'll be nothing serious happen to spoil this record before next July. Felt better walking to school on the first chilly morning of the year with snow reported on the higher Pennines.

The day punctuated by medicines of various kinds to keep me going but a very busy day and consequently a difficult and tiring one, especially when feeling a few degrees under. The sight of 25 Classical Studies books each containing around two sides and which will require substantial correction was depressingly daunting. So easy to set easier-to-mark homework or none at all, as I'm afraid some colleagues do, while others such as R——— and P——— are so very conscientious and especially Jack who, I must add, after 37 years is still so very hard-working.

I wonder how many books I have marked in my career? I do regard it as very important; as I tell the pupils, "It's that intimate moment that we share, you writing to me and I to you." I must remember to have that seminar with the ITT students before the present batch leave.

Interviewing Year 11 border-liners (ie D/C grades) again today. First one, a strange lad, pleasant in many ways, but the Nazi/anarchist/violent graffiti inside his exercise books was alarming. He dismissed it when I raised the subject but I'm certain he is into National Front activities and sympathies.

Jack and I [were] called outside at lunchtime as there were again undesirables on the premises.

An irate phone call from a parent this afternoon as Clive had not yet responded to his complaint of bullying. He says he has faith only in Mr Bush. It was embarrassing and he was difficult to convince that Clive is a very busy man.

Badminton (wife: "How can you be ill if you can play badminton?") and Careers Convention until 9.00 pm.

What a week!

[1] *Time flies very quickly*

Friday 17th November 1995

FRIDAY at 5.00 pm ought to be a special time: another week is over, beef and red wine to come and our closest friends the Griffins visiting tomorrow night. Unfortunately I have a dreadful cold and a music/drama evening at school tonight. It is F———'s first and he deserves every ounce of support.

My day started at 4.45 am. Bad throat and sneezing so downstairs for hot milk and aspirins. A very busy day ahead. If I had stayed off, it would have created more problems – or so I tried to convince myself and wife.

Year 9 Classical Studies to begin the teaching day although I marked some books left over from yesterday before school started and I still haven't finished the pile. Despite my feeling so many degrees under, I taught the bottom set well. The way I felt, it made me slow down, speak slowly and take things calmly. The result was an enjoyable lesson for both parties. What do I conclude from that?

Taught Year 11 scansion of Roman verse for the last time and ready at break for coffee and paracetamol. All set to mark at 11.20 am but called down by Clive to be a witness as he dealt with a very aggressive parent defending his own guilty son. Clive's legal training stands him in excellent stead on such occasions.

This was followed by the second Year 11 interview. He is an able boy but is underachieving by a long way and he is fully aware of it, or so I believe. He will do well but why is he taking on 10 hours a week at £2 an hour in the local supermarket two weeks before his 'mocks'?

Lunch hour taken over entirely by planning next week's activities with Clive, our head of music and the vicar from Almondbury Church. Things are looking very promising. It meant a rush to full assembly for us both. Called in by G—— to subdue a Year 11 Breadth Studies class. Like mice when I left but next year?

This was followed by complaints from our Head of Year 7 about pupils simply not doing as they are told while she's on bus duty. She has to be there as Head of Year. There were no problems last week while I was there in the rain but I worry about this for they should be able to cope.

The day finished by being able to report how pupil Y—— who had been taken away by her teacher parents to another local secondary school and had blamed KJS for her causing numerous problems, is causing even bigger ones now that she is in Year 11. We believe we were right all along!

Monday 20th November 1995

I'LL begin Monday morning with Friday evening last. End of a wearying week, feeling quite ill yet came home at 10.15 pm feeling uplifted. The music/drama/PE Department dance evening was inspirational. Superb compere and the performing arts team working very much as a team – and the pupils excellent to the point of bringing me to tears. I shall miss these aspects of school life enormously for just so rewarding to see these pupils in such a different light ...and dress. One seen on the corridor for misbehaviour every day revealed talents of staggering depth.

It also makes me realise how much I miss those extra-curricular activities of earlier days – sport/scouts especially. One learnt more about a pupil in one muddy week at camp than in perhaps two or three years of classroom teaching. It's a great loss that extra workload/more commitments have meant teachers are less able or willing to take on such activities – a sad reflection on current educational trends.

To today which has been full of ups and downs. Some good work marked, some shocking graffiti written on the walls of the boys' toilets. Not obscene but will take much cleaning off. Main culprit identified from his signature on his pencil case. He'll be scrubbing for an hour to-morrow night.

A very unpleasant incident at the weekend which resulted in a girl's hair being cut off in lumps at an unsupervised party – drink involved! 14/15-year-olds and it all spills over into school. Police involved. Where are the parents and their responsibilities?

Management meeting concern about two staff who are not doing their job. Clive to intervene but not easy to pin them down. Easier in industry no doubt?

Positive note: Kirkheaton buses to bus bay; slow in arriving but generally all went very smoothly. No overcrowding and nobody left behind.

Tuesday 21st November 1995

Physically slowly improving although by lunchtime I did begin to feel drained and at home I felt quite exhausted for the first half hour. Mentally a more satisfying day for despite feeling weary, I had an upbeat lesson with Year 9; plenty of amusing asides and another solid chunk of Virgil covered with Year 11 – they are a delightful group whom I shall miss very much.

An envelope for Clive which I noticed on his desk had details on the outside which indicated within were the Kirklees 'League Tables' based on GCSE exam results. KJS fourth equal this time – slightly down as we knew it would be but still in the Premier League. The trend is clearly one of better schools getting better and the worse getting worse, as well-motivated parents opt for the 'better' schools. This is an inevitable trend and I'm thankful I am at KJS and not, for example, at Rawthorpe which is probably doing an excellent job in very difficult circumstances.

The main business of the day did not concern me. Clive is still following up repercussions of a weekend incident outside school. More details provide more alarming evidence of parental indifference and neglect. Consequently the school has to pick up the bits, wasting many hours of time and much energy which should be devoted to educational and not social matters; or can we separate the two? Has the school's role now become interventionalist in domestic problems? If so, we need more time and training.

I took the Year 7 assembly on their own for the first time. Circumstances have meant I had missed the previous two. Welcomed them to KJS in their 11th week and read to them about Founders' Day celebrations and descriptions of the first Taylor Dyson procession up St Helen's Gate 66 years ago after assembling round Big Tree[1].

A distressing note on which to finish. The Bursar informed me with acute embarrassment this morning that according to a tree surgeon Big Tree itself is to come down. It is in a dangerous condition. Is she still playing her prophetess of doom role or am I biased and sentimental?

[1] *'Big Tree' was an ancient sycamore tree, with a slatted hexagonal seat around its trunk, located in the main school playground. Believed to date back to at least 1820, it features many times in this diary.*

Wednesday 22nd November 1995

THE first three lines of yesterday could have been also written today although I believe I'm not the only one suffering. The yellow slips for staff cover, written in Jack's immaculate hand, seem to increase daily and two more were added at lunchtime. Why are some staff regularly off and others hardly ever? Pain barrier and thresholds? Determination? Stubbornness? Chance to shorten the week? No way of ever telling. It's the pupils who lose out, of course, and it's they too who in some ways reflect the above. The most able are hardly ever away while the least able... It can't be purely physical. How about a PhD relating absence to IQ, to sex, to year etc? Could be an interesting thesis here. Now there's an idea for retirement.

Enjoyed my two lessons in the morning, one double and one single. At last, I feel I have begun to strike up a relationship with Year 9 Classical Studies but it's been hard work.

Management [periods] 5 and 6 discussing how to manage an experienced teacher whose relationship with the pupils seems to be deteriorating still further. The domestic problems are well known too and disliked by the pupils, some of whom will probably have experienced in many cases such things themselves. Teachers ideally should be role models of stability in the home but very sadly they mirror much of today's unstable society.

Managed 15 minutes practice with Jack and W—— for tomorrow night's carol service and then half an hour with the Head Boy and Head Girl practising their contribution to the OAS dinner and Founders' Day service.

Periods 7 and 8 were spent with the ITT student teachers. Had introduced 'marking' as my theme but sidetracked happily – for it worries them greatly – into maintenance of discipline and the teachers' nightmare of losing control and not being able to cope generally. They are doing very well and pupils whom they find difficult are the same ones whom very experienced staff find the same.

The third evening of new bus arrangements. These are going well but the buses are still arriving too late. Phone call at 4.15 pm from a father complaining about damage to his son's cycle. He is threatening to go to the police.

He is a policeman.

Thursday 23rd November 1995

TODAY was 'Pastoral Inset Day'[1] or at least morning from which I opted out. Wisely and usefully, I later discovered. Jack described the three hour session as 'long' but then so are he and I – in the tooth. Illness severely affecting staff and C——

being delayed in traffic meant we were short of cover so I finished up buzzing around the school, remote controlling and acting as student teachers' mentor in order to keep things running smoothly, which they did for the most part. How does one judge if Inset is offset by improved performance and results?

The policeman father had indeed contacted the police. Fortunately, I interviewed the pupil at 8.35 am and at Clive's request rang the father to reassure him. He took it all very calmly but I couldn't contact the Police Youth Liaison Officer who seems to have been given the impression that KJS is a seething bed of theft and petty crime. Theft comes in waves. At the moment it's quiet but in general we fortunately seem to have little in comparison with some schools.

Stayed out of the Bursar's way today as I thought she interferes in so many areas of school life where I don't feel a Bursar should enter. But then again am I out of touch? Ancillary staff are no longer etymologically well described. W——, IT expert now, can certainly teach staff a few tricks and he is better than many with some pupils.

Gearing up for tonight, tomorrow and Saturday – hearing speeches and improving readings. I shall be so relieved when I wake up on Sunday morning. Quick sing at lunchtime.

Interviewed three of our most able pupils; very humbling to acknowledge that they are far more able and gifted than I am or ever was.

Popped out to watch the School First XI versus an Old Almondburians' XI football match; 1-1 at half-time but school lost 6-1 eventually despite excellent play from such young boys. Ten years ago or fewer I might have played. How much I enjoyed those games.

Next preparing for tonight's Founders' Day[2] service when I shall sing in a trio and read from the school history – especially the section which requests that 'the school may be a little bit different from any other school.' My favourite passage and so meaningful now.

[1]*Training in aspects of student welfare. 'Inset' is a contraction of 'INSErvice Training Days', originally known as 'Baker Days'.*
[2]*Because of the growing size of the school, King James's held two church services at this time to mark its original founding on 24th November*

1608. In 1995, the first – for senior pupils and members of the Old Al-mondburians' Society – was held on the evening of 23rd November and the other, for – Years 7 and 8 only – was held the following afternoon.

Friday 24th November 1995

TODAY begins with last night for, of course, it was Founders' Day evening service as mentioned last thing yesterday. Wonderful service, shame about the congregation. Some 60 performers involved in the choir and orchestra, 12 staff present and probably 40 to 50 others; parents of Head Boy and head girl and a few parents of the performers. Fewer than double figures from the Old Almondburians despite personal invitations. The future of the service must be in doubt. What more can we do? The service opened with Andrew Froud, the vicar, singing plainchant. He was preceded by two acolytes in almost total darkness. It was pure theatre and to believers very symbolic. Parents were dropping children off to pick them up 40 minutes later. Are they so anti-church or religion? Our singing went well and I found my voice almost breaking as I read with deep feeling those words from Taylor Dyson's farewell speech to the Old Almondburians in which he talks about preserving the character of the school. Shall I be able to find a speech of equal worth? Sincerity will be no problem. The gathering afterwards in the church hall was most convivial.

And so to bed and up again at 5.00 am, mind a-racing. In school by 8.10 am marking and still have not really caught up. Taught two good double lessons. I say again how Year 11 Latin are such a lovely group and say again how much I shall miss them and wonder if they will equally miss me.

I, in consultation with Clive, decided to leave my 'Announcement' until after the main governors' meeting on 14th December at which I hope my redundancy will be approved. Will the news break before then? Apparently, the rumour sweeping KJS at the moment is that Clive is retiring and I am taking over as head. Lunchtime was very busy, tutoring the readers for this afternoon and mainly getting material out for tomorrow night. A few disciplinary cases to deal with and one in particular was infuriating in that it involved damage to our new litter bins which cost £200 each.

At 2.00 pm we were on our way up the hill for my last Founders' Day Service. It went very well indeed. Years 7 and 8 only but still meant the church was full to capacity. Andrew Froud's burning of a £10 note certainly gripped the congregation's attention at the beginning of the service. Back to school in the rain and buses were all away by 3.29 pm. The first wet evening but then we need the rain. Tomorrow I shall be in school by 9.30 am along with others to help set up the bar and make other arrangements for the OAS Dinner which will [probably] not finish before midnight!

Roll on Sunday morning.

Monday 27th November 1995

I MUST really go back to Saturday as it was/is so important a day in the school and my calendar: OAS Dinner day. It began at 9.15 am, opening up the school for delivery of bar necessities. Managed to set the alarm off, again. Shall I manage it before I finally depart? Back at 2.00 pm to help setting up tables etc and then again at 6.30 pm as chairman of the OAS to welcome guests and oversee operations.

General opinion seems to be that this was one of the best-ever Dinners. Lively, amusing speeches and no one really overindulged. 153 attending, 108 bottles of wine/port consumed, 288 pints of beer/lager and then add on the spirits. Who had my share? Had to keep sober. My speech was well received, or so it would appear, but I was pleased by 11.45 pm to slip out, the excuse being to take Rev Andrew Froud home as he had a sermon to preach next morning. I confessed my plans for the future to him on the way home. I felt so relieved and I need to unburden myself to somebody. He is such a delightful fellow. Next morning, Sunday – thanks to *Nytol* and exhaustion – I did not wake until 9.15 am. Almost unknown for me.

And so to Monday. I'm still not feeling well. Nationally there's a 'flu epidemic. Spent first hour typing up an account of the weekend for the

School Annals and newsletter. Alarm that a Year 10 pupil is missing from home with his girlfriend. It will be in the local paper tonight. Police are going to call. Apparently his father walked out last Tuesday and moved in with new girlfriend. When will something be done about the cruelty to children? It makes me very angry.

While supervising for R—— I confiscated a passage being written by a Year 11 [pupil]. The sexual perversions and language contained therein were very disturbing. She is a very bright girl. Photocopied this material and sent it to parents, remembering their defensive attitude adopted two years ago. I am intrigued what their reaction will be.

This afternoon, nearly three hours of management: two hours of theory, 20 minutes with the buses and then 35 minutes on what I might call practical issues. Can't help thinking we've got the balance wrong or is it me suffering from cynicism brought on by tiredness and old age?

Tuesday 28th November 1995

TRAINING DAY. Left for school some 15 minutes later than normal. Usual humour along the very well worn theme of "Isn't it a lovely place without kids?"; "If only it were as quiet as this every day!"; "Schools are great places – pity pupils spoil them". Actually I found it depressingly quiet – missing children already?

Clive and Pat talked to staff on SEN[1] policy; time passed very slowly although they were very good. I am convinced my retiring is the right thing to do at this stage. Cynics among the staff, and there are plenty of them, were eager to turn any discussion into "What are we (ie you) going to do about 'The group from Hell?'" This is an actual quote.

The most interesting part of the day for me was a visit by three people researching their family history. I was able to help them by finding a reference to the great-great-great-grandfather in school in 1851 and a mention of his father too.

Wrote to Gerald Hinchliffe, author of *A History of King James's Grammar School* and told him of my plans.

Lunchtime meeting with Pat, Clive, Jack and B—— to discuss the recent Year 11 interviews. Actually, I found this very interesting as we have common themes and lively ideas flowed. Timetable '96/'97 discussed with C—— and L——.

A governors' staffing subcommittee meeting tonight. Here's hoping they recommend redundancy to the full governing body.

Runaway pupil mentioned yesterday was on the front page of the *Huddersfield Examiner* tonight, resplendent in his KJS uniform.

[1]*Special Educational Needs*

Wednesday 29th November 1995

BACK to reality! After generally dry and bright days, this morning proved a typical, dark, dank day in late November. Spirits, strength and yes, enthusiasm sink as the term progresses and low feeling is exacerbated by a persistent cold. I'm going to school practically in the dark, spending all day inside in artificial light and coming home at 4.45 pm in the dark. No chance of therapeutic gardening and even the *Daily Telegraph* crossword will have to wait tonight until I've marked some GCSE comprehensions.

Apparently last night's staffing subcommittee unanimously recommended to the full governing body Clive's new management plan despite one member having embarrassingly naive and unfounded qualms about the procedure by which redundancy is offered. The next obstacle and presumably the final hurdle will be the full governors' meeting on 14th December.

There was an incident yesterday on buses from town involving our pupils confronting an ex-pupil. Even on days when not in school are we expected to investigate? Surely this is a police matter not a school one, although I will probably investigate it tomorrow. No time today.

Two satisfying lessons and then an unusual situation involving interviews for a new secretarial post. The three 'would-be's' had to sit in and take notes while Pat, Clive and I discussed my report on yesterday's curriculum team meeting regarding the '96–'97 plan. Very technical and I felt for them – or at least two of the three who have never worked in schools. At 4.30 pm there was still no decision despite their having been here since 9.30 am.

Had lunch with the candidates and then a number of disciplinary matters to sort out. Particularly concerned with one Year 11 boy, very weak academically but certainly not physically. He will learn little more while at school and would be far better off doing the job he is guaranteed when he leaves.

In Year 10 assembly, the theme was 'ups and downs' which seemed to go very well. 40 minutes with the ITT students on 'marking and the return of books'. One of my favourite themes.

The buses were the fastest away yet and then to a Year 10 team meeting with E—— in the chair; she is very good. I was there to watch the would-be, disenchanted wreckers. It was lively, enjoyable and positive. "You are so clever," said E——.

Flattery? But we all need that periodic, positive bit of stroking!

Thursday 30th November 1995

A MUCH better day in so many ways. The weather is the same but at last I am beginning to feel better mentally as my physical state slowly improves. More energy, more bounce, so much so that I was able to indulge in some MBWA this afternoon. This was – as always – illuminating, interesting and generally appreciated. However, I did sense in most lessons that staff and pupils are becoming tired, while patience and tolerance are wearing thin; there are still three weeks to go before the Christmas holidays.

All teachers agree that, of the three, this is the most demanding term and the one in which most work is done. Whatever happened to the four term year which once seemed imminent? It has so much to commend it.

Today was satisfying in that there were numerous, comparatively small tasks to accomplish which I seemed to do with alacrity and efficiency both lacking in previous days. The Year 8 books, top set Latin, however, cause concern. There are still too many where the work is so badly presented even from the girls who are so often much the neater. Why is so little emphasis placed on presentation these days? It must start in the primary schools.

The interview with the Year 11 girl *(27th November)* was at 1.10 pm. Having met the mother two years ago when she was somewhat aggressive,

I was prepared to be stubbornly defensive myself. No need. B—— sat in with me and made some excellent contributions. Both father and mother were very grateful, supportive and concerned. What a worrying situation for them. A very bright, undoubtedly university material girl, is (as B—— put it) at the crossroads. Turn left, she is into drugs, sex and a low paid job. Turn right and she will go to Greenhead College and University. She is keeping non-academic company. Which way will she go? Hope I manage to record it.

I have one such in my Latin group. Her work is going downhill and she may spoil my last results if this continues. Sharp words tomorrow.

The Unwind Club seemed in a cheerful, positive mood after school. A pleasant way to conclude a satisfying day.

CHAPTER 4

December
1995

— Snow! —

Friday 1st December 1995

IT'S rapidly approaching one third of the year gone and it really doesn't seem that long since 1st September. Yet those sun-tanned teachers of the new term are looking decidedly worn and drawn. I sense, too, [that] the pupils are weakening physically and mentally. There are still large numbers absent as coughs, and colds abound. There are still nearly 3 weeks to go in what, we often agree, is the hardest term.

Friday night, 7.30 pm: a wonderful meal; Jumilla followed by Rioja; and a word with grandson Jordi on the phone. All this meant that the day assumed a belated but genuine rosy hue.

Another very busy day which started with Clive in my room about 8.15 am and finished in his study with the same topic at 4.45 pm. Really no break throughout the day, so 8½ hours more or less non-stop. Main concern is the staff who feel that the school's discipline is slipping and want the topic on the staff meeting agenda for next Monday. This request seems to come mainly from those who find maintaining discipline 'challenging'. Clive [had] tackled B——, a new teacher with wide experience including London. He finds KJS pupils marvellous – cheerful, well disciplined, motivated and [he] sings the praises of the management team. He insists he is not wishing to be ingratiating.

It's all relative. Many colleagues from other schools in our locality would find KJS to be so; it's a question of where one sets the levels of acceptability and exam success.

It took me half an hour to get going this morning with reduced Year 9 CSD[1] group but in full flow with Year 11 Latin and amusing them with my attack on ITV's weather caption last night. 'Very wintry extends it's (sic) icy grip '.

Various miscreants sent to me at lunchtime but comparatively minor misdemeanours. Year11 pupil, academically weak, bored and raring to leave, came up with more sensible suggestions as to how to keep him out of trouble than we have ever suggested. Out of the mouths of babes and sucklings and Year 11 supposedly 'thickies' but obviously not this one!

Two weeks of new bus arrangements. Nobody left behind, no overcrowding and no complaints. Bliss!

[1]*Classical Studies*

Monday 4th December 1995

YESTERDAY sickness, splitting headache and dozing most of the day. The only intake of food, which did not return, was one meat pie about 9.00 pm. Today I was at school by 8.10 am. Why? As Margaret always says, "You're only ill at weekends." As Old Almondburian, Gordon Kaye[1] once told me when I asked how actors keep going when they must feel ill at times, he replied: "Dr Footlights takes over." An element of this I suppose. I did sleep reasonably well and felt distinctly better on waking this morning as usual at 6.50 am. Began to feel a bit weak by 2.00 pm but better at 5.30 pm with two hours' Spanish evening class on the horizon. I really don't feel bad at all.

Enough of this indulgence in self- analysis. What kind of a day? Not bad at all actually. Year 11 are on the first day of 'mocks' which always seems to alter the atmosphere around the school. I managed to prepare Year 11 Latin paper and have almost finished duplicating it myself. As with most tasks, they are – like hills to climb – far greater when viewed from the bottom than when the climb is underway and a steady rhythm established.

Pat and I met to discuss Clive's 'snow advice'. Two to five inches forecast for tomorrow. This is early. Let's hope it doesn't reach us. Drought and snow to contend with at the beginning of December is a bit much. I can just imagine parents – all the fussy ones – sharpening their telephone dialling claws.

Lunchtime, one or two minor disciplinary matters to sort out, but generally quiet. Met with the secretary and head of school kitchen to have a debriefing on last week's OAS Dinner and make notes for '96. I felt a real fraud as I said, "next year we must do this..., next year we'll have to have..." etc. Still two weeks and they should all know the plan. What a relief it will be.

Staff meeting until 4.20 pm and then furthe   r debriefing with Clive and Pat. Considering how I felt yesterday at this time, as I said earlier, not a bad day at all.

[1]*Gordon Kaye, star of* 'Allo 'Allo!, *attended King James's Grammar School from 1952-58; the popular comedy actor's stage name was Gorden Kaye*

Tuesday 5th December 1995

SNOW! Not a lot, but sufficient to create frissons of excitement among the pupils and I suspect some staff as any disruption to routine is a diversion to many. By 3.00 pm, despite flurries, there had been no phone calls at all as far as I had heard. By 4.00 pm there was a light covering and temperature dropping. Tomorrow there may be more worries as the forecast suggests worsening conditions. It comes at a bad time in the term as Year 11 are doing their mocks and Years 7 and 9 are also taking national tests so already there is disruption to the daily programme. The last thing we need is patience becoming strained and spirits becoming lower. So much easier when things are running smoothly.

Taught a sound lesson to Year 9 and then down to Clive's study to discuss curriculum changes and mainly last night's staff meeting. There were seven groups who made jottings and comments. As predicted, having put like with like, some groups had adopted a positive approach while others were highly negative. How interesting (or coincidental?) that the new teacher who claims these pupils are the noisiest she has ever worked with is herself becoming notorious for her high-pitched screaming at her classes. Clive is becoming very agitated and seems bent on some strong language to the moaners and cynics. Good. Now let's see words turning into actions.

Year 11 hard core a real problem when not in the exam room. I'm very disappointed that the pupil from last Friday, with his sensible suggestion regarding future conduct, behaved very badly both inside and outside the exam room. Was he genuine last week or pulling the wool over my eyes? Or just – and most likely the case – cannot prevent himself from being a thorough nuisance.

Intense 40 minutes with C—— and L—— over timetable documents and then feeling guilty as I left at 2.45 pm for a building society appointment in town. The first time out of school early since…?

Walked home in the snow!

Wednesday 6th December 1995

LEFT school last night at 9.00 pm after chairing my last meeting of the OAS. The meeting had been moved from the Huddersfield Hotel because of the pressure on space there pre-Christmas. The weather was awful but the attendance reasonable, the atmosphere lively and plenty of wit and conviviality. Quite sad really for I have increasingly enjoyed the office and believe immodestly that I have ameliorated the situation and relationship between the school and the society; this was critical last January.

This morning's main worry was possible loss of voice. I was up before 5.00 am, coughing and spluttering and unable to get back to sleep. I've never lost my voice in 34-plus years and I don't want to suffer that indignity at this late stage. My voice, my weapon and proud possession. Such an attribute in teaching and if it were to go it would make national news, as I told Year 8 who smiled tolerantly and indulgently.

Year 9 CSD are certainly improving and the latest test results are much better. However, there are still some whose attention easily wanders.

Gave a Year 11 girl some private tuition for 20 minutes. She is struggling. I hope it's my advice she seeks and not my company. One cannot be too careful and again at this late stage, I don't want any scandal. Teachers are so vulnerable in these situations and that's such a shame for relationships of the right kind when built up can lead to inspired performances and renewed efforts.

More planning with T—— and W—— over tonight's meeting.

Year 8 rebellious pupil with whom I do believe I have a good relationship, strained it at lunchtime. He refused, pleading injustice, to wipe tables when requested to do so by an LTA. I took him out, asked him to do it for me. He was not happy. 20 minutes later he changed his mind. A calm, persuasive approach had triumphed over force.

I gave our ITT students a little apostrophe test. 26 were required in a passage and the English graduate found six.

Buses in the sleet and then to the curriculum panel meeting in the freezing ODH[1] until 4.45 pm. A constructive meeting but I sympathized with T—— when he exclaimed, "When will they stop changing things?" "I don't know, T——, but any changes won't affect me!' I thought.

[1] *The Old Dining Hall was built as a schoolroom in 1848 and is one of the oldest parts of the school.*

Thursday 7th December 1995

ONE third of the year already gone. It's akin to life. In some ways I seem to have been at King James's for an eternity; in others it was only yesterday when, as a student teacher, headmaster Harry Taylor was suggesting wearing a gown to give my youthful looks some added authoritative weight. So with the year. It's a long hard term, that I know, but in other ways 2nd September – my birthday and a sunny, optimistic start to the term – seems very recent.

Snow! A little more overnight but sufficient to add excuses for non- school uniform, snowballing in forbidden parts, slush on the corridors, two broken windows – all problems well known to teachers, but more of that anon.

The day began with no sign of Clive, held up in traffic on Penistone Road, as were others. It's a good job I live sufficiently close to school to walk. Even in the worst weather I am there (I write yet again immodestly). It's true though that those who live near the premises often have to hold the fort until those from the outlying districts arrive. These are problems peculiar to hilly areas such as ours.

Voice just about holding out during Briefing and Year 8 lesson. First real chance to get out and about and see the ITT students in operation. For the most part they are doing well, but even in a school such as ours they have a tough job securing the tight discipline which is essential for a teacher establishing him or herself. One week to go and then they have to go off to another school and start all over again.

Managed a little sing, or rather croak, for the three-part *Good King Wenceslas* carol which we are hoping to sing at the carol concert.

Investigating the broken windows. Herd behaviour again and glass showered on a girl's hair. Rather rough on pupil C——, one of only four and therefore easily distinguished black pupils in the school. He appears to be a prime mover but all will be seen tomorrow. Blame and costs to be evenly distributed.

Bus duty tonight was in bitterly, creeping-damp cold but pupils remain good humoured thereby ensuring a cheerful, disciplined end to the day.

Friday 8th December 1995

CURSE the snow! It's comparatively light but certainly makes life more difficult. The pupils seem on a permanent high. Jack reports that huge groups were roving in out-of-bounds area, showering others and then taking refuge among staff cars and certainly making themselves late for registration. Four or five of yesterday's Year 11 ringleaders were singled out for punishment.

Yesterday's broken windows saga saw 11 members of the group responsible lined up and willing to pay £1 each to meet the cost of repairs even though the real culprit has now emerged. This was a plus. "Can I pay now? " said one, producing a £10 note.

Test for Year 9 CSD was easy but they struggled as they just cannot remember facts and details. My fault? Have I ever really come to terms with teaching the very weak pupil? Have I ever attempted to teach them to memorise details? The actual lesson they seem to enjoy and I have no problem in bringing delivery down to their level.

Year 11 are an excellent year but there is a hard core of disillusioned boys, eight or nine of them, who are not taking 'mocks' seriously and causing D—— , and indirectly me, a real problem.

A set three French pupil, a police inspector's son, told D—— he was not going to come in for the higher level listening next week. D—— was furious. The same arrogant lad refused to remove a ring yesterday. "Impossible to remove it". Given soap and told he would stand outside my room until it was off. One minute later he returned, ring removed. Today it was on again. His father rang at 4.15 pm. I was half expecting a complaint. In fact, he was worried and supportive and he wishes to come in next week. The boy sees himself as a sporting prodigy with no need for qualifications. Compare [him with] Jonathan Dyson, former Head Boy and Huddersfield Town footballer, with a degree in finance and who remains so modest and delightful. How much this boy could learn from him.

The week finished on a positive note in that the classes visited were being well taught in an orderly manner. The buses arrived promptly and were boarded in a cheerful manner. When the last one leaves it's just like putting the children to bed and coming downstairs.

Monday 11th December 1995

TO school in the dark and home in the dark, drizzle, cold and snow still lying, mist verging on fog. Hardly uplifting but home to open fire, Christmas lights and the tree put up yesterday. These things do inevitably have an effect on one's attitude to pupils, staff, and teaching in general, especially as the end of term approaches.

The penultimate week, and by one week today 'The News' should have become public. What a great relief that will be! The day began with a Year 8 supergrass reporting damage to a bus seat on Friday evening. Investigating this has taken up quite a good proportion of the day. As always the net widens as one digs deeper; what a mixed metaphor! It's difficult to allocate blame. Shamelessly, I had a video of Presentation Evening 1991 on my desk. This, the miscreants were led to believe, was from the bus company, special delivery this very morning. So confessions tumbled out. How to punish I have yet to decide.

Year 11 Latin 'mocks' 8.40 am to 10.00 am. Started marking them. A real disappointment in some cases but as always they will improve by next June; plenty of practice needed.

A Year 9 pupil from my Classical Studies bottom set, always cheerful and pleasant for me, has been truanting – £100 withdrawn from his savings account and spent on beer and the like. He is in company with a 20-year-old man. The parents are devastated. Another solitary, unhappy Year 9 has redness round his nose I must mention this to pastoral Pat.

Thanks to *Nytol* and the fact that at last the cough seems to be subsiding

I was able to make plenty of positive contributions in our management meeting.

The arrogant youth from last Friday is reluctant to accept that he is so. He has refused any private tuition from R—— should it be offered. We'll see his father after the 'mocks'.

Tuesday 12th December 1995

Slightly milder, the snow has nearly all gone but grey and damp weather reflect the mood around the school. Even effervescent C—— said, as she gave me a lift home tonight, everyone seems to be becoming ratty, short tempered and is walking around like grey zombies; that's a very fair description with seven teaching days to go.

With this in mind, I reflect that I have previously said that the penultimate lap is always the hardest in the race. Next Monday the end of term will be in sight. Then it's a sprint to the finish and a flop at Christmas. Only a few days after this, we shall all begin to feel human again.

This same theme applies on a wider scale, for I feel that the last academic year – ie 1994-95 – was harder than this one, as I can now say "that's the last time I shall have to..." and not "next year at this time I shall have to...".

Year 9 Latin was hard going this morning and it ought not to have been. Again I can suggest just tiredness on the part of teacher and taught. I noticed Little Miss Nose Stud again and thought that she's now gone a whole term without compliance, the only one. Another word from me before Christmas?

Main job at the moment on the teaching front is marking the Year 11 Latin GCSE 'mocks'. A real mixture, for some good students are disappointing and they will need lots more practice. However I certainly have one of the best-ever students in D——; she is in the Bryan Hopkinson class. She achieved 133 out of 146 on an 'unseen'[1].

The bus seat damage will result in letters of apology and some reassurance to the bus company ie I may have to end it there.

A quick lunch and started an exam at 1.10 pm. Meeting with A——— and T——— this afternoon. Clive wants us to see if we can plan a new 25-period week timetable for '96. More change and this will not go down well with some teachers. He's also upset A——— by taking over a project she was planning. I feel he may be trying to help but it's not wise and perhaps he needs to delegate more.

The last 45 minutes of the day were spent with the police inspector father. Clive suggests we should not tell him that in our view he has been spoiling his son but the father readily admits he can no longer impose his will on him. The arrogant son ended by saying he had little intention of doing any revision tonight.

[1]*A passage, usually prose, which the students had not previously seen as opposed to their set texts which were translated together in class*

Wednesday 13th December 1995

YET another grey December day and not helped by a poor night's sleep. Partly self-induced in that we went to dinner last night at the home of David Shires and his wife of six months. He runs a [garden] nursery at Totties[1] and is a former pupil. It was a delightful yet salutary evening.

The food and company were excellent but it's important to realise (a) that other people out there also lead a very tough life, with hours much longer than those of teachers and with much insecurity forever hovering around. At least teachers have almost 100% job security. And (b) how influential teachers are in their pupils' lives. I know it's stating the obvious but, as I think I've said before, the odd throwaway remarks – be they condemnatory, laudatory or amusing – are picked up by pupils, stored and given worth far greater than we teachers can ever imagine. The tales [David] told revealed this yet again.

And so to today, feeling very weary and it was a real effort to gird up my mental loins and teach a good lesson to Year 9 and Year 8 Latin. But I did manage it and could almost feel my energy draining away like water disappearing down the plughole.

More marking of Year 11 which I had started at 8.15 am, and a long discussion with Clive and Pat on various domestic matters. The local newspaper is pestering us for a story someone had fed them about a confiscated knife. This is real gutter press stirrings after the murder by stabbing of a headmaster in a London school last week[2].

The police reported a Year 11 pupil who had switched off the bus engine last night by opening the emergency cover at the back. "Do you want us to prosecute?" Indeed we do but surely it should be the bus company's decision and not ours.

The last sessions with the ITT students. How tired they seem and are! I have to reassure them that this is normal but that hardly helps them to feel any better and I have to say it's always going to happen at the end of the autumn term.

[1] *Garden Centre at Holmfirth*

[2] *Philip Ambrose Lawrence, an Irish school headmaster, was stabbed to death outside the gates of his school in London when he went to the aid of a pupil who was being attacked by a gang.*

Thursday 14th December 1995

A VERY significant day in that the governors have their full meeting tonight to approve – I hope – the management revised structure for '96/'97 and my redundancy. It's deep breath, fingers crossed time. An easier day at last and inevitably that guilty feeling when one is not under so much pressure as usual.

Completed the marking of Year 11 Latin exams. A real range of marks for an able group: 41% to 95%. As every year there are some real disappointments, inadequate revision and great gaps on some papers and yet as usual by June the standard will have risen and I hope the Ds will have become Cs at least. There will have to be some hard talking done next week, however. I've always promised them success but if they are bent on examination suicide then that's a different matter.

Two lower school pupils whom I suspected of truancy yesterday – and whom I asked B—— to investigate and follow-up with a telephone call – had not been followed up by 12.30 pm. What is more they had not brought in absence notes. I rang. Truancy in both cases. Spoke to B——

and strongly suggested he take more rapid action in future. "Let them know we are on the ball." He seems willing enough to take the hint.

Still no chance to sing even though we are supposed to be performing next week. The *Huddersfield Examiner* is still pestering us; [so] "not available", "in meeting" etc. Will they ever give up?

Real dilemma post-1.30 pm when I was handed some obscene material written by [girl] pupil N—— and passed on to a boy. It had been confiscated by W——. This girl has a notorious mother who plagues the school. The daughter wept copiously when confronted. She has, she says, lost or had stolen a personal stereo and is desperately trying to raise £40 to replace it before her parents find out. Not sure how this is connected to the obscene writing. She has an extremely pushy parent who puts her under great pressure, this we know.

To inform or not to inform, that is the question. I am going to sleep on it and decide with Clive's advice what action we should take tomorrow – which will not be just another day!

Friday 15th December 1995

THE day in some ways began last night at about 9.30 pm I was in the *Woolpack* at the end of year OAS badminton club party – 12 of us in the village hostelry so closely associated with the school for so many years. Staff governor E—— came in for a pint or three. He brought the news that the meeting was over quickly and smoothly and the new management structure approved. A wave of relief and optimism passed through me.

By 2.45 am I was up again for I couldn't sleep. Fast asleep at 6.45 am when the alarm went. Clive was in my room by 8.15 am with 'The News' but, of course, I had to confess I knew. He wrote to Oldgate House today confirming the governors' decision; now I have to wait to see if they give approval for redundancy terms.

Taught lessons 1 and 2 without realising that next week we shall be on holiday at this time ie they missed out on the lighter vein lesson.

Rang 'Mrs often-very-difficult M——' concerning yesterday's letter. She came in at 1.00 pm and Pat joined me. She was on the defensive and very concerned. How complex the situation is and how difficult for parents bringing children up in these liberated, promiscuous times! I do feel an enormous generation or even generations gap here. Saw the daughter later on and was very disappointed. I thought I had smoothed things over for her but saw now much more of the rebellious child [who was] far from grateful. So much for my good intentions.

For the first time for some time, I lost my temper with a Year 10 pupil who had been truanting earlier and with whom I have spent some time. This morning after 15 minutes he assured me of his fervent wish to obey the rules. He skipped Assembly this afternoon and was found hiding in the shrubbery with three others. Why? Patience and perseverance are waning.

Now to Monday and 'The Announcement'. Clive seems almost more uptight than I am. A weekend in Billingborough to visit mother will be an escape.

Monday 18th December 1995

HERE I sit at 5.30 pm, having had a brandy in my coffee and a glass of 'reserva' red wine from a bottle brought to my room at 8.30 am by the S——'s. Feeling relaxed and racing through the *Daily Telegraph* cryptic crossword. A sudden realisation that I hadn't yet written up my diary, and "on this very special day" as Margaret said. I suppose it's because I am so relieved although I do feel yet again emotionally drained. The news was broken between 1.10 pm and 1.50 pm and any other happenings were dominated by the build up to and climb down from those – to me – momentous 40 minutes.

The day did begin at 8.35 am in a predictable way with a father in reception to complain about the bullying of his daughter and asking me to become involved. A sad case which I think I have managed to sort out, but we shall see.

Meeting with Clive and Pat to discuss the format for today's lunchtime. Clive had telephoned Oldgate to make absolutely certain that all was in order after receiving his letter last Friday. "Yes, all is fine, Mr Bush should receive a letter before the end of the week." More tension. I told Lesley, head of the school kitchen at 9.30 am. She was upset at my going. At 1.10 pm Clive had called an extraordinary staff meeting for an important announcement. All staff appeared to be there. He explained the governors' approval of the new management structure and then he handed over to me. I spoke for about 4 to 5 minutes, really from the heart. I feel it was well received but some colleagues looked stunned. I left the staff room almost immediately to prepare for my revelation to the school. Assembly had been split between Key Stage Three (Years 7, 8 and 9) and Key Stage Four (Years 10 and 11). I spoke briefly to the younger ones who sat in absolute silence. Then I went upstairs to Years 10 and 11. More or less the same approach but this time there was clapping and cheering which colleagues said was genuine and appreciative. I suppose I had feared it might have been their showing relief but apparently not. Stayed out of sight for the rest of the day.

This evening to my Spanish class for a Christmas party.

Tuesday 19th December 1996

IT'S 10.15 pm! The fact that I have only just realised that I have yet to complete today's diary must be very significant. The reasons are twofold. Firstly, and more likely, I have felt very tired again today although a little less drained form of tiredness, if that is imaginable and that has continued into a busy, pre-Christmas evening. More likely, and secondly, it is a feeling of relief and considerable anti-climax after yesterday. The situation is reminiscent of the day when we learnt of Mike Thornton's death last April. Head of English, Mike was a very popular staffroom figure of some 20 years' standing It had been a sudden death and news of same was on the answerphone at 8.15 am. The staff were shocked but by break conversation was returning to normal in the staffroom, by lunch chattering and by 3.15 pm laughing and joking. In the hurly-burly of school life the pace at which life moves on means there is little time to sit around, mope, ruminate and surmise about death and retirement. Or that's my self-assuring reflection. There have been warm words of reassurance that I'll be missed and it won't be the same school without me but generally life has continued smoothly on this antipenultimate day of term.

Year 9 Latin saw a lively quiz with which to finish and then to my special Year 11s. "Now, my precious little ones, you know why you are so very special!" "Aarrr" they chorused, sounding genuinely very affectionately moved. Their exam papers were very mixed but I remain optimistic that all 19 will gain a 'C' or above in the June exams.

Completed Year 11 reports.

[At] lunchtime I was planning, along with 11 other volunteers, for the last-day-of-term quiz. As always, the same colleagues are taking on the extras which add so much to school life while there are those who sit, feet up in the staffroom.

Met with A—— and D—— to discuss the '96/'97 curriculum but felt so tired the session was cut short. A 25 minutes' spell of bus duty in the cold drizzle was sufficient to clear the head.

Home comparatively early. Two days to go. Roll on!

Wednesday 20th December 1995

ONE day to go to the end of this so long, so tiring term. Those sun-tanned, relaxed faces of early September have turned grey, worn and drawn, even haggard in one or two instances; all rather alarming. There are exceptions. Some of our more laid-back colleagues seem to manage to maintain their relaxed miens but they are the exceptional minority.

Despite this, a feeling of bonhomie seems to have pervaded the place. The more recalcitrant pupils have apparently begun their Christmas break prematurely and staff were generally in very good humour today as they turned the ODH into a dining room as in days of yore. Tables were laid and wine glasses filled in many cases – not *with* many cases! This was Christmas Dinner Day and the kitchen worked its annual miracle. They have fewer staff yet served up over 500 meals. Senior staff ate with the pupils and then I had a sing with P—— and Jack which went very well.

On a more mundane note, I had to deal with four Year 10s guilty of graffiti on the stone in Fenay Quad. Red marks on our beautiful stone –

what an eyesore. They have been scrubbing with wire brushes and nearly all is off. To be completed tomorrow.

Also at lunchtime four or five Year 7s were pushing a reluctant, diminutive youngster into a fight with tearful results.

Year 8 Latin and Year 9 Classical Studies both enjoyed my usual end of term house quiz on subjects going back to last September. Enjoyed by both sides of the classroom. This afternoon toured a number of rooms and generally a cheerful, orderly atmosphere. Colleagues are tending to approach me quietly and individually to express sadness at my going, to offer their support and to state they believe that I am "doing the right thing."

Thursday 21st December 1995

CHRISTMAS carols playing, fire blazing, Christmas cards scattered over the settee. These are from teaching colleagues, ancillary staff and pupils; quite a pile which I shall not have next year.

Threats or promises of snowfall during the day had added a frisson of apprehension and excitement to pre-school planning. By 8.20 am, one mother had rung in to say that she was not sending her daughter to school "because of the snow." In the event there was barely a covering and it had turned to drizzle by the end of the school day. Generally the day has gone well although I do feel very weary.

It's the staff dinner tonight. I shall be there as it's my last. On reflection I have felt more tired when younger. I distinctly remember being almost physically sick with tension and exhaustion, and then not really feeling human again until the New Year.

By 9.00 am I was in the sports hall for the House Quiz and apart from a break at 10.30 was there until 12.30 pm. The first part was for Key Stage Three and the second for Key Stage Four. Questions of a serious and light-hearted nature and some physical activities. The noise level was very high but good humoured and colleagues were most helpful. My old house, Jessop, in the lead by some 25 points after the first session and finished up eventual winners by a single point. Great excitement.

Senior staff ate with the pupils while the rest had their own special lunch in the staffroom. Some singing practice at lunchtime and then back-to-back assemblies, a Christmas service with 25 minutes of readings and some carols from our staff trio. Pupils were excited and noisy between the items, a far cry from the formality of the 'Nine lessons and carols' of the grammar school days.

Are children no longer able to sit quietly? Watching children's TV occasionally, it is clear that unless they are leaping up and down noisily they are not having a normal life. To teach them the pleasures of quiet, thoughtful, relaxing activities would be very beneficial; or is this nostalgia-wallowing from a tired, out-of-touch, soon-to-retire teacher?

Friday 22nd December 1995
(TRAINING DAY)

CHRISTMAS BREAK

CHAPTER 5

January
1996

— Bus problems – and Little Miss Nose Stud —

SPRING TERM

Monday 8th January 1996

TRUDGED somewhat heavily to school. How dare I after such a long break? A whole week into the new year was a most welcome, longer than normal rest. I had needed it and I'm sure so had all my colleagues. I did feel the benefit although not 100% recovered from last term's heavy cold.

The morning was very dark and drizzly – not conducive to putting a spring into one's step on the first day of my last Spring Term and it was with some apprehension that I began my final calendar year. The nagging worry whether I shall retain interest, enthusiasm and efficiency until 19th July persists.

However, such worries are swept aside as soon as I sit down at my desk. I had been in school last week but Urgency bears down upon one as the bell rings and hustles one into almost frenzied activity. Time for brooding is/was non-existent. Three ITT students arrived by 8.30 am. So important [that] they are made to feel warmly welcome, two from Huddersfield University and one from Leeds Met; all seem very keen and eager to please. Two are football fanatics so a bond was immediately established there.

Had a quick trip round corridors welcoming people back, "Happy New Year"-ing and then ploughing through my in-tray which seems to have a fresh piece of paper in every half hour.

The new Head's secretary seems delightful, although I must remember not to make hasty judgements – one of my failings. Give her a term and then judge.

First growl of year to pupil who had been rude to dinner supervisors. Tears flowed. Too hard? Management meeting from 2.00 to 4.30 pm. Enormous amount of work covered and I felt alert and fresh. How long will it last ? Sent out for the last five minutes by Pat, Clive and Jack. What are they plotting? There'll be more of this, no doubt.

Tuesday 9th January 1996

ALTHOUGH the chart I keep which shows sunrise/sunset indicates that at least mornings are becoming lighter, this one was the darkest yet and it marked my mood to a certain extent. The first two lessons of the new term were hard going. My fault or theirs? The former I feel, for I found it hard to rouse my enthusiasm even though I knew that this would be the last time that I share the sadness of the class at the death of Caecilius and Cerberus, victims of Pompeii's eruption, in the Cambridge Latin course.

So much depends on the teacher's enthusiasm in this education game. The two classes are very pleasant groups but even Year 11 Latin proved a disappointment. I suspect I was depressed by the absence of the two students who can least afford to be off. Isn't this so often the case? The top ones are hardly ever missing. Are they never ill or do they have the determination to struggle on when not 100%?

After break, I felt even more down, for the amount of work piling up seemed almost overwhelming. The result was that the tight feeling began to take hold. In the Latin lesson I could not bring the term 'asyndeton[1]' immediately to mind and then searched my own room without success for some pupil-produced translations. Then I remembered I had had them duplicated last term and found them on the appointed shelf in the staff room, awaiting my collection. This was a cheering relief. However, it does make me realise that I am perhaps at last beginning to lose my super-efficient tag which I believe I had and I am grateful that I shall not have to soldier on to [age] 65. How did they manage previously? Not the same pressures, I'm sure.

Ten minutes' sing at lunchtime helped and successful timetable/curriculum planning session. Buses are rescheduled but more of this tomorrow. Tonight is the Annual General Meeting of the Old Almondburians' Society when I shall hand over my gavel and plaque as I step down from being chairman. Another job completed.

[1]*A stylistic device used in literature and poetry to intentionally eliminate conjunctions between phrases; for example, 'I came, I saw, I conquered'*

89

Wednesday 10th January 1996

BY far a much better day even though it's been a very hectic one. A number of factors helped: (a) last night's handing over of the OAS responsibility was a relief and symbolic; (b) the morning was much lighter, in fact definitely light by the time I reached school; and (c) at last, I have contact with Janice Whelan at Oldgate House who apologised for lateness in getting my letter out but said I was to take the call as confirmation that I would be leaving under redundancy terms. The amount is still being calculated but I would certainly be offered the higher of the two schemes for premature retirement. Great news. We shall open the champagne when written details arrive. How do I feel about this? Any guilt? I'll reflect and hope to comment later.

Bretton students – four due this morning. Number 1 rang at 8.15 am: "Queasy stomach – not coming today". Number 2: "Bus problems" and arrived 20 minutes late. Numbers 3 and 4: on time. One student, a male, has a long ponytail. Does it matter? Would certainly count against him with some people in a job interview.

Two lessons this morning went so much better than yesterday and it's difficult to say precisely why. As ITT co-ordinator I ought to be able to do so but, as is often the case, there is a strong element of unpredictability that makes analysis far from easy.

Lessons five and six with Clive and Pat discussing the need for an immediate or at least a quick decision on how to advertise the new senior teacher posts. It was interrupted by Pat being called out to a Year 11 girl who had overdosed. A very troubled background. What a change from the cheerful soul I taught in Year 7. The changes from 11 to 16 are still for me often staggering in both physical and mental make up. The ambulance arrived at the same time as last term's run-away boy's parents. He has had difficulty in re-entry. All this caused me to have to cut short my ITT seminar.

Buses better but still not good enough.

Thursday 11th January 1996

I'VE just realised that I don't know the outcome of yesterday's overdosing [incident]. That really is not good enough. Am I slipping? I feel so, in view of what happened at 10.00 am.

I received a phone call from my close friend, the vice-principal at Greenhead College, Peter Griffin and almost immediately another one from ex-head of French, Dave Gregson. A tap on the door at 10.20 am from a part-time teacher found me on the phone. "Shall I cover your class?" she offered. Gulp! I had come to school convinced it was a non-teaching day and that after one term of having a Year 8 Latin single at 10.00 am!

It so vividly reminded me of N—— whom I have mentioned before[1] as typical of a teacher declining in esteem and efficiency in his final years. The standard joke was his saying, "Is it *that* time? Oh well, not worth going to class now." If I went on to 65, I suspect I would be the same or even worse. And in how many others have I seen the same symptoms? That's why I'm so pleased – and I hope wise – that I'm finishing in July.

Marked a set of books – routine but satisfying especially one which was an outstanding piece of English from a Set 3 boy who has such low self-esteem. After 35 years [I'm] still able to experience a buzz!

At break, Clive in near panic. The deputy headship advert at Almondbury High School was on the local bulletin. Would H—— be applying and throw the interview plans into confusion? I spoke to the person concerned who assured me that the intention was to stay at KJS and apply for a senior post. Her great attachment for the school and a real desire to see pupils' success was clearly apparent. Very welcome news to senior management ears.

Lots of minor disciplinary matters to sort out over lunchtime which I felt I handled well and really enjoyed. Matches found among junior pupils and paper being lit under the stairs was somewhat more serious. Big warnings.

Must record that the buses were away in driving rain and in record time tonight. Managed 20 minutes' sing at 4.00 pm and there is hope that R—— will be rejoining the quartet.

[1]*17th October 1995*

Friday 12th January 1996

VERY pleased it's Friday evening and shortly we are off to *The Three Owls* to celebrate confirmation, though still only verbal, of my eventually receiving redundancy payment. Pleased also that it's Friday evening as I have felt very weary today. Mostly self- inflicted in that two hours' badminton last night left me physically drained and that feeling was still there this morning after too short a night's sleep.

Enjoyed my first lesson with Year 9 bottom set. Year 11 Latin was disappointing. There were so many loose ends to be tied up before the lesson properly began. Virgil continued – they do find it hard and it's difficult for the lesson to become little other than a spoon-fed lecture. They are too self- conscious to make many positive contributions. Nevertheless, I exploded at one point – which I have hardly ever done with this set – when one girl sat immobile as I made a very important point. She was obviously far too distracted to make any notes. I did apologise to her later in the day but she seemed not to have taken it to heart and had not been offended. She acknowledged her mind was on something else. Knowing the lifestyle of these youngsters and their home situations which are often so volatile, it's not surprising that their concentration is not always 100%.

The rest of the day was one of those 'bitting and piecing sessions', as I call them.

The build up to Presentation Evening, and my last major public appearance, is now taking up more time. A phone call to Andrew Taylor last night secured his services as presenter of prizes. That's one big step forward.

A major case of bullying to tackle on Monday. Noticed the overdoser in assembly appearing normal despite her trip to hospital in the ambulance and staying there overnight. How they 'live'! And how ordinary my school days were.

Monday 15th January 1996

ALTHOUGH the mornings should be getting lighter, today it was gloomy in the extreme as I tried to adopt a steady pace through the fog. The days of the early '60s, when visibility was sometimes almost nil, are no longer the case. Closure of mills and smokeless zones have brought about a transformation in industrial towns such as Huddersfield.

Despite the weather I felt better than last week – it's just getting started. All hills look less steep once one has begun the climb and it's always surprising how far one can climb in a short time once underway.

Before 8.30 am I had been handed two notes, one from B—— requesting my investigation into a possible theft during his lesson last Friday and another from R—— who had seen two boys on one bike with no lights riding down the steep St Helen's Gate which is not permitted.

And therein lies the dilemma. I need to wean colleagues off seeing me as a troubleshooter/sorter-out-of-all-manner-of-problems and to pass matters on to Heads of Year. However, I do enjoy this aspect of my work – ego trips? – and I don't want colleagues to think I am abrogating my responsibilities and becoming demob-happy. I have always said that this is my great fear. I want to go out at the top or at least on the level.

Met with Clive and Pat for over two hours this morning discussing the procedure for the new senior posts appointments. Almost there. Within four weeks and two days they should have been appointed.

Generally, I feel that the year is going well but I would like to know more what my senior colleagues think about my going and what approach they believe I should adopt. Possible meeting over an evening meal is planned. Clive and Pat were out this afternoon so Jack and I comprised the management meeting. Most of the time spent discussing KJS after my retirement this year and Jack's retirement in July 1997.

We wonder...

Tuesday 16th January 1996

HOW unpredictable. How illogical. Tonight I feel physically quite fit and mentally quite alert and spiritually quite cheerful and yet, I shouldn't. I have tried not to let family matters creep into my daily recording of events and often one has to shut out personal concerns and problems and get on with the job of facing a class or participating productively in a management meeting. Teachers do have homes and families which pupils often have difficulty in imagining.

My opening comments were prompted by Sunday night phone call from Margaret's mother who has a 'shadow' on her lung and from a daughter who has possible health problems. And thirdly my hip nags – variable but usually I am aware of it.

Yet, despite these three things, I taught a good Year 9 lesson and a better Year 11 Latin than last week and that was after a two-week holiday when they were comparatively poor. The next half hour taken up with Clive discussing his drawn-up details of how [candidates] should apply for the senior teacher posts. I do think he is making it very time- consuming for candidates; they have to write an awful lot. Six people have so far picked up details of the requirements. I predicted five of them, my sixth still to do so. Will he? Two are clearly Clive's front runners. Many, many hours have gone into this process. If he gets his two favourites, then the cynic in me suggests it has all been rather pointless.

Saw a pupil at lunchtime about his late dinner money. How minor when I hear his background – he has been brought up by grandparents, having been rejected by his parents when young. Teachers have homes, so do pupils. And we expect them to conform.

Theft from bags at lunchtime. Excellent work from B—— meant the culprits were found, most money recovered and punishment to be decided.

Six buses here at the same time, a record. One late so we were still delayed.

Wednesday 17th January 1996

STILL gloomy meteorologically speaking but generally another bright day scholastically. I was relieved to see the boy who was in detention last night as firstly, he had not informed his parents and secondly, he had walked home. They were supposed to ring me this morning. How much do they know? I shall have to try to contact them again.

It seems that Clive will exclude [yesterday's] four thieves for three days. Lessons with Years 8 and 9 went well although I sense I am taking the easy way out with the Classical Studies ie giving more notes and insufficient exchange of ideas. Latin will always be – sorry, has always been – my forte and first love. I am still 100% convinced of its enormous benefits when well taught.

Train of thought; saw B—— about the future of Classics at KJS. This conversation, although it was in fact a brief statement of facts from me, was approached with some trepidation on my part. I was basically informing B—— that pupils do not find those lessons particularly enjoyable and unless there is a change in approach or style, especially more humour shown, then the subject will disappear from the timetable. I do believe that a sense of humour is one of the prerequisites for a successful teacher and I have frequently said that unless there has been a genuine laugh during a lesson then that lesson has not been a complete success.

Called upon to take the first full assembly on a Wednesday. My first assembly of any kind this year. Hubris raises its head once more? 'Wanton and insolent arrogance' is the dictionary definition. Well, I thought it was a good assembly. Up to 750 pupils in silence, listening apparently intently and not a whisper as I left the hall. What control and yet when I'm leaving there's a great sigh of relief – disguised, of course – because there's always the lurking fear that it could all fall apart.

Three-quarters of an hour with seven ITT students. Again I feel the session was enjoyed by both sides.

And then one bus very late. Back down to earth.

Thursday 18th January 1996

This is a first! Filling in my diary at 10.45 pm having suddenly realised that this daily duty had not been done. Year 11 parents' meeting to blame. Very long day in that I was in school by 8.05 am and left tonight at 9.15 pm with two hours off around tea, after which I took Margaret to Greenhead College, where she teaches, for an open evening.

The day began with my talking with Clive and updating him on yesterday's events. He had been out at a meeting and then he was delayed this morning which meant [I] had to take Briefing. Jack came to ask me to cover B——'s lesson, for he had gone home feeling very ill. Jack had warned the class that I was coming. There was hardly a sound when I got there, a top Year 10 geography group.

My compliments passed on to Year 8 Latin. Although, in theory, the equivalent of the Wednesday group, I usually enjoy this one less but this morning it went very well and I had to make up for missing it last week. Did some 'looking in' periods five and six.

Reprimanded a Year 7 girl: multi-ear-ringed and finger-ringed. Mentioned her very short skirt, which resulted in floods of tears. "Income support" etc mentioned. I melted. Should I have done? Tears can be a very useful weapon for chipping away at stony hearts.

Note from member of the English Department: "Could you please ammend (sic) your report. You have omitted the grade." Discussed with B—— the difference between 'emend' and 'amend' and he, mathematician that he is, produced the different Latin roots. The English teacher would have had not the slightest interest in or knowledge of such matters. Sign of the times. I shall miss such linguistic exchanges.

Buses late because of traffic jams and roadworks.

Year 11 parents' meeting brought the first real feelings of emotion as gratitude expressed and regrets mentioned. "Can we persuade you to change your mind?" "Won't you stay until her brother in Year 8 is through King James's?"

No chance! Alea iacta est[1]. The Rubicon has been crossed.

[1] *The die is cast*

Friday 19th January 1996

SEVENTEEN weeks of the academic year have slipped by and on writing today I thought how soon I shall be reaching the halfway point. Life in school, I reflected at some point, goes on just the same in that I don't alter my approach in any way whatsoever and have made no attempt to slow down. Having said that, the approach in Classical Studies is perhaps different in that I indulge in more notetaking which the pupils seem to enjoy but could be construed as an easier option on my part.

The handing in of Latin homework this morning by Year 8 brought an original excuse. The gist of it was: "Dear Mr Bush, my daughter could not complete her Latin homework last night as she was kicked on the head by her horse and spent most of the evening at Huddersfield Infirmary, having her head checked." Certainly a problem I and my contemporaries didn't have when tackling our homework. A pity I have not kept all the 'excusal notes' I have had over the years. They have often brought originality and amusement.

Felt Year 9 Classical Studies and Year 11 lessons went well. First Year 11 Latin, of course, after last night's parents' meeting. Clear from the atmosphere that my positive conversations had been passed on to offspring and I am still optimistic that they will produce a marvellous set of final results for me.

Routine marking after break broken up with some MBWA. T—— and I had a sing for 20 minutes at lunchtime. Despite yesterday's extended day, I felt livelier and it went well – even the Welsh now seems possible[1]. I have never known such a linguist as T——.

During the afternoon looked into every classroom. I was impressed. This is the first Friday we have had tutorials rather than full assembly and I feel it will improve the atmosphere.

Roadworks still causing buses to be late.

Chat with Clive and home by 4.40 pm.

[1] *The leader of the quartet had no problem with Welsh and could sing the Welsh national anthem better than most Welsh people. He gained a double first from Cambridge in French and Spanish.*

Monday 22nd January 1996

DARK days continue. My record of sunrise and sunset times suggests we should have 10 minutes of extra daylight in the mornings but today dawned darker – is that possible? – with sleet and a biting east wind. It does make life within school more difficult. As I passed along crowded corridors today, I did picture the summer term when pupils can spread themselves on our delightful school grounds. Certainly spirits rise at such times but that's a long way away. January is a depressing month; next year shall we be able to spend it in some warmer location? A pleasant, certainly fulfillable dream.

Monday morning began very quietly. A few pupils brought late books, one or two reported to present themselves in correct uniform but otherwise a very calm start. Did a cover for period two and then a phone call from a parent wishing to see me urgently. It seems this was occasioned by a mother who, at last Thursday's Year 11 parents' evening, had expressed her anxiety over her daughter's friendship – a very long-standing one – with another girl who was leading her astray by "intimidation". I listened but she seems to have taken my silence as supporting her case. The second mother, politely and pleasantly, queried this. This really is a problem outside school and I'm not prepared to separate them within it. The former, I feel, is being over protective and restrictive but it's difficult for me to be too blunt. I don't envy such parents when today's teenagers are under such pressures and temptations.

Spent 11.00 am to 12.30 pm with Pat and Clive discussing the analysis of the GCSE 'mocks' results. In the afternoon I went with C—— to Deighton School to listen to the problems of Design Technology in the national curriculum. I tried to be involved and interested but have to admit that I am pleased that July is approaching.

How complicated school life is compared with 20 years ago.

Tuesday 23rd January 1996

A VERY positive day! Why? As has been said before, a good night's sleep does make an enormous difference. I think I shall have to advertise *Nytol*. How I sympathise with insomniacs especially those that have a very demanding, no-hiding-hole job to do the following day.

My day began with a letter from the Busbys. Gerry was a former and very popular mathematics teacher with whom we thought we had lost contact.

Positive too because at long last the official redundancy offer letter finally arrived, its date Tippex-changed. This is great news and more financially than I would have dared to hope a year ago. I think of other long-serving teachers who did not get a penny and I feel guilty to a certain extent. Then I think of others in the private sector with enormous golden handshakes and I feel only a twinge. I shall have done/given 35 years with only 5 days off. Will it stay at 5 or am I tempting fate? Really I have given so much of my life to the school, for many holidays and weekends were surrendered in earlier years to sporting and scouting activities. I think of those times and then I don't feel so bad. It will certainly help to bridge the north/south gap in terms of housing.

Feeling fresh and buoyant and then promptly forgot the day had been advanced by five minutes; consequently five minutes late for lesson one. Taught Year 9 Latin too hard and almost over their heads. After 35 years still making mistakes but at least I am prepared to self-analyse and admit my error. The work has suddenly become much more demanding. Year 11 were a delight, as is normally the case. Completed Virgil with Turnus's soul winging its way to the Underworld. How appropriate.

Lunchtime pastoral meeting. Later working with B—— and L—— on curriculum planning. A long talk later with Clive regarding the last two days' events and then discussed the celebration of my departure to be held in July.

Whom to invite? What a list!

Wednesday 24th January 1996

A VERY busy day indeed, one of those when at times I did not know which way to turn. No major crises or catastrophes but one of those bits and pieces days again when interruptions, phone calls, knocks on door and two meetings at the same time leaves one feeling drained. Then tonight we are out for an early evening meal with Walter Raleigh[1] and his wife so there is little time for reflection.

A major leak above N1 meant room changes to be arranged hastily, including my own class. Year 8 went well. Some genuine hearty laughs which is always an uplifting moment in a lesson and then to Year 9 Classical Studies. This had been moved to our temporary laboratory and the atmosphere was strikingly different. I wonder if anyone has done a PhD on room arrangement and ambience and how classes react to the conditioned behaviour in a certain room. I know that in the labs with certain teachers, classes are allowed to be chatty. This does not suit my style of teaching and I was not happy with today's atmosphere. There was no question of losing control but I did not feel at ease. It made me reflect on those colleagues for whom maintenance of discipline is a problem and how wearing, how morale and energy sapping daily confrontation must be. Why do they continue?

A reassuring 'Future of Latin and Classics at KJS' meeting with members of the languages department.

ITT seminar again went well but there are a couple whose lack of sparkle worries me. It is difficult to see them ever really being great successes in the classroom but they will pass/qualify.

Bitterly cold bus duty and K.78 late yet again.

[1]*Fellow teacher*

Thursday 25th January 1996

SOMETHING noteworthy happened yesterday and I cannot remember what it was despite recounting it to Margaret on arriving home. That is to say, I failed to record it last night. Therein lies a recurring problem: how to note such events in the course of a very busy day.

Today I have again felt well and the day passed by busily and generally pleasantly. A bitterly cold day with a temperature never above freezing and a biting wind giving a wind chill of -12°C according to the weather report.

Made a slightly late entry into Briefing to muted coughing and my embarrassment. A pile of marking but even this was pleasantly routine. How many books have I marked in 35 years? Yet I still experience a thrill when a pupil suddenly reveals talent, or annoyance when another is underperforming.

Year 8 Latin went well although two girls who had copied had a public rebuke. I felt sorry for them but I'm sure they and others will think twice before doing it again. I often surprise myself by my ability to detect copying. A mistake in one book is remembered perhaps 20 books later when it is repeated in another pupil's homework.

Lunchtime saw a steady stream of pupils to my door, sent by the lunchtime supervisors. The bitter weather seems to lead to more misbehaviour round school but there's really nothing particularly serious.

Ah – remembered! Yesterday, rounding the labs, I first smelt and then saw a group of smokers. Cigarettes hastily hidden but not hastily enough. Some were smoking others were not. The 'Ireland finger-sniffing test' was applied. Ken Ireland, retired PE teacher, claimed to have invented the test and had proved its infallibility. The pupils were called to my room one by one. The first was guilty, the second had sprayed on deodorant as had a number of others. Those with no smell were deemed innocent. A series of confessions and sent off to Head of Year 10. One had stuffed a packet of cigarettes down his sock. Why do they always smoke Regal?

An after-school talk with Year 9 tutors and careers officers regarding preferences.

Bus duty! The K.78 arrived at 4.07 pm, nearly 1 hour late, claiming roadworks and jams on Wakefield Road. We cannot leave the pupils so the unions are now becoming involved.

I am in a union too.

Friday 26th January 1996

THE drawn curtains revealed in the darkness steadily falling snow. This, in combination with a Friday, was bound to cause Trouble. The phone was soon ringing with the usual "Is the school open?" "Are the children being sent home early?" "A and B will not be coming to school today because of the snow!" There must have been all of one inch by the time I arrived. Some more during the day but nothing to cause 'Snow Chaos'. All the buses arrived on time and they all left on time. The K.78 was the earliest it has been for some time. How pathetic! Some pupils went off at lunchtime. We must follow this up rigorously on Monday.

Even more worrying and a possible cause for closure of the school was the fact that Clive's computer has been emitting smoke. This is his own and will cost much to repair. He uses it 95% for school work but has to pay for it himself. Something amiss with such a system.

Year 9 bottom set Classical Studies severely depleted. Year 11 top set Latin all there, 19 out of 19. What conclusion does one reach? I had forewarned Year 11 that two Year 7s would be sent to me by C—— at the beginning of the lesson for a '3B': Bush's Big Blast. They are a noisy, difficult-to-settle, class and I had 'ordered' C—— in their presence to send me two in the first five minutes for committing the most minor offence – even fiddling with a pencil! Nobody arrived. At break he said "I could not find the slightest thing to fault. I even left the classroom and on my return there wasn't a sound!" Such fearful respect or respectful fear? They'll miss me. Such arrogant pride!

Lunchtime sing with R—— re- joining us at long last.

Clive seems to be sympathising more with Pat and with me in our view of our Bursar.

The end of a busy but generally satisfying week. Halfway to half term,

Monday 29th January 1996

MONDAY morning syndrome has never been one of my problems in teaching until recent years, and then the symptoms have not been severe. Yet this morning a combination of circumstances caused me to feel low, generally disgruntled and short tempered. I felt annoyed with myself in that the problems were minor. "Think of A——," I told myself. "Over the weekend she has lost her little niece whose life was spent mainly in the operating theatre and in intensive care." My circumstances? Car battery was absolutely dead, so problem for Margaret who needs to leave by 8.10 on a Monday morning. So a taxi for her and our mechanic, Barry Fella, contacted this afternoon.

Bitterly cold and paths were sheets of ice. By 8.15 am complaints coming in regarding snowballing a double-decker and snowballing near school windows. Friday afternoon truants seen in cases where I was involved. Parents ringing up "Is the school open?" Incredible really, as all main roads are perfectly clear.

Bursar has news that Big Tree is to come down at half term unless a second opinion can be obtained to the contrary via a qualified forester. Rang Gerald Dobson in Scotland whose son is the Balmoral Estate forester. So moves are afoot.

Little Miss Nose Stud appeared and I sought to persuade her to comply with school regulations. Not optimistic. A personal letter from a former KJS Head Girl whose son is in Year 9 and having various problems. I'll try to help her as a friend rather than Deputy Head.

Took Year 7 assembly and ranted about snow and all its unpleasant sides. I then had to apologise to our [appropriately named] Head of English, Jay Snow, a Year 7 tutor, who was smiling benignly.

A two-hour management meeting and found my concentration wavering at times. Weather or old age? Time to move to a warmer, less demanding climate.

Tuesday 30th January 1996

SO much better! Barry Fella had sorted out the car last night, even putting it to bed in the garage. I had to get it out again as it was Spanish evening class night. Felt much more cheerful this morning as I walked to school as a slow thaw perhaps matched my mood. Nevertheless, eight Year 11 snowballers near staff cars to see before Briefing.

The lessons were enjoyed by all parties this morning. We are making our way through Cicero's 'Ethics of a Salesman'. As we are having our house up for sale before long – Cicero deals with this topic – it means that I can resonate with and personalise this subject, much to Year 11s' amusement. Little Miss Nose Stud has obviously chosen to ignore my personal plea. Saw a Year 11 pupil who was in minor trouble last week. I am reminded that his mother is very seriously ill and they are living in a caravan at the moment. This all puts one's own problems again into perspective. The burdens some youngsters have to carry!

Managed a lunchtime sing for all four of us and we produced an excellent sound – quite exciting really.

It seems that school PE sweatshirts are in danger of replacing pullovers. Must stop the rot. E——'s voice failing so she asked me to do the reading for her in an assembly. She was kindly complimentary afterwards.

Planning tomorrow night's Curriculum Panel which I shall be chairing and about which I feel a little apprehensive.

A one-hour meeting with Clive and Pat. We, especially Clive, have real problems with R——'s declining health and W—— who has been reported for allegedly having struck a pupil. This means both could eventually face dismissal or departure. How glad I am not to be a Head. His burden is onerous in the extreme. Could I have carried it?

Wednesday 31st January 1996

PHEW! Pleased when the clock reached 4.30 pm for reasons to be explained later. Snow, bitterly cold weather and the attendant problems remain. They seem to serve as excuses for late arrivals, non-conformist dress, and staff illness especially among lunchtime supervisors. Again, I think of summer days, when pupils can stretch out on the grass during breaks. Everyone is then so much more relaxed.

My main concern today was that Clive was away all day and any problems and crises would have to be shared between Pat and me. Three within the first half hour. Year 11s snowballing last night inside the bus; mother concerned over Year 10 'beaten up' by some Year 11s yesterday when snowballing had developed into an assault and she was demanding to know what action was going to be taken. A Year 8 was hit in the eye with a 'snowball' which was now an iceball. Why did we not ban all snowballing? We had had the opportunity in a full assembly. Six pupils from Rawthorpe on the premises at break and a resultant fight.

In between all this we had an enjoyable Year 8 Latin lesson and satisfactory Classical Studies with Year 9; the latter seem to need and appreciate a harder teach. It's still a pleasure to escape to the classroom. Pupil S—— remains a real problem. He has difficulty exercising self-control. The ITT students and I agreed how a single pupil can completely dominate and influence the atmosphere of a lesson. He really needs special treatment.

Lunchtime taken up with visitors to my door, usually sent by the LTAs. I kept the lower school back [after Pat's assembly] to investigate the snowballing of a horse and a man opposite the school gates. Mildly amusing in its way but serious in others. I suppose as there was a horse in-volved, the supergrasses were happy to supply names.

A particularly satisfying session with the ITT students and then on to the Curriculum Panel as chair. Apprehensive even at this late stage in my career. There were 15 lively minds there, some far livelier than mine and always there's that lurking fear of not being 100% in control or caught off guard. Actually, I felt alert and by regularly dropping humour into the meeting, the atmosphere was clearly helped. Left on a high.

CHAPTER 6

February
1996

—"Big Tree could stand for many more years" —

Thursday 1st February 1996

TIME 6.00 pm and off to badminton. As I was late home and so mentally drained, I thought it wise to leave today's entry until my return, most probably physically shattered but mentally refreshed and thereby able to see things in a more balanced light. (Can light be balanced?)

That's better. Now 9.30 pm. A heavy defeat by Peter Griffin, my long-time friend and badminton opponent, in the first game followed by revenge in the second. Easier doubles, hot shower and finally I have 'mens sana in corpore sano[1]' again or at least a little 'sanior' than earlier. As I told the ITT students, teaching is a very demanding job at the best of times and if one is not feeling 100%, especially physically, it becomes even more demanding and stressful.

Today was one of those times when I felt occasionally overwhelmed. So many people to see, phone calls, interviews and at the end of the day discussing the seven applications for the two senior teacher posts. There are going to be some unhappy people around and I have been given the job of doling out the Kleenex and the comforting words.

Interviews with Year 8 pupils were the most time-consuming but most rewarding part of the day. They usually only confirm what we know goes on in the classroom but, as indicators of our interest and a spur to greater efforts, they are invaluable. The pupils do seem to value them.

W—— assault case seems set to run while at lunchtime I had a violent phone call from an irate parent about a non-school jumper. The offer of a secondhand one brought near apoplexy at the other end of the line! Two invasions by Rawthorpians, rumour of a knife and a visit from the Rawthorpe Deputy Head. There is now a ban on snowballing yet it is still happening.

I have picked up the Telegraph crossword as an escape.

[1]*A healthy mind in a healthy body*

Friday 2nd February 1996

OH DEAR! What angst my impending departure is causing! Clive was asking to see me before 8.30 am to unburden himself over last night's meeting of governors. They were faced with the unenviable task of reducing the seven applicants for the two senior teacher posts to four. It seems that the governors are looking for a 'hitman' to replace me as they feel discipline in the school is already on the slide and in September will become worse.

The trouble is, I can understand their worry. In my opinion, Clive is keen to appoint theorists and the three who didn't make it, L——, R——and M——, are potential disciplinarian boat-rockers[1]. He is going to face a divided staff and some very disgruntled senior people.

I am so sad that it's turning out like this but it was predictable. He wanted me to talk to the Chair of Governors after school but I really don't want to get involved. The three unsuccessful ones were to be seen by me. I have seen two but I couldn't find L—— "who is furious".

It has generally been a very busy day. Phone regularly ringing, interviews for Year 8, two double lessons taught and pupils 'to see' although I am trying to send more and more to Heads of Year.

There seems to have been few chances for humour recently although I do try to bring some into lessons.

At last, completed the claim forms for the confiscated ring which was lost while in my possession. A couple of positive calls thanking me for help. Such calls are so much appreciated.

An excellent sing at lunchtime, all four of us being present. The first bus duty of the week and not too late away.

Home by 4.15 pm feeling really tired, as during the afternoon I had raced through a number of routine jobs to move them on before the weekend.

Roast beef tonight with a strong red wine. Already feeling better!

[1] *Were keen to see a firmer disciplinarian regime*

Monday 5th February 1996

MY final year's fulcrum at break, 11.00 am to be precise, as the balance tipped gently, the second half of the academic year began and the descent down the gentle slope started. I do so hope it will be mostly smooth. Please, no major upsets or illness.

Still very cold, very icy and 'severe weather warning' being trumpeted by the media; already pupils are anticipating disruption. Felt quite buoyant as I slithered up the slopes – that is for a Monday morning.

As I left on Friday, a message was coming through from Grasscroft about "outrageous behaviour by our pupils." They were iceballing a brand-new car and I was to follow this up today. I did at about 11.00 am and the lady was very reasonable whereas I was furiously ashamed. This will be followed up in assembly on Friday when I should take the whole school.

Spirits were lifted considerably by a letter from a last year's pupil who was requesting tickets for Presentation Evening. She was a constant problem and we clashed frequently. [Even] if I receive no more letters on my retirement, that one would suffice. It spoke of respect, appreciation and always-to-be-remembered. I shall treasure it but as the 'non-replacement of a hitman' discussion rumbles on, I dare not show it to fellow senior managers.

Another nose stud has appeared – why can we not take a strong line on this? – and, knowing the parents, it is likely to stay.

More complaints over B——'s lack of marking. He has never done much but his condition, suspected Parkinson's, prevents it now. Again, how much longer can the situation continue?

Management meeting followed by pastoral meeting. Clive seemed to agree to a stay of execution for Big Tree. OAS to pick this up tonight.

I shall be at my Spanish class. Bus duty in the biting cold but the buses were away in reasonable time.

Tuesday 6th February 1996

I SHOULD have mentioned that yesterday began with The Law. A police car was driving round the back of the school as I arrived, as there had been a break-in into the kitchen with resultant disruption.

Last night, on returning from my evening Spanish class, I was greeted by Margaret with the news that I was to have visitors within a few minutes. Dr E—— and son in Year 7, a neighbour and acquaintance over 30 years, arrived at 9.30 pm to explain how the boy, one of only a few of a racial minority in the school, had systematically been subjected to extortion over many months. The result was that he had handed over many pounds – perhaps up to £100 – which he had stolen from home.

My wife Margaret's reaction was "poor little chap, how cruel!" Mine was "keep an open mind". Margaret, bless her, has no such experience. Having dealt with, dare I say, hundreds of 'cases' over the years, one learns to be sceptical and to avoid jumping to temptingly obvious conclusions. The father was in school this morning as Clive investigated the matter for much of the day. It appears the child has lied and was giving away money, gifts and cigarettes, possibly to curry friendship. The matter is ongoing but the father is not going to like the conclusion.

Taught two really good lessons. In full flow with Year 11 and they enjoyed it.

More complaints over the Science department and P—— in particular. The atmosphere is tense before tomorrow's senior teacher interviews. Whatever the outcome I sense that there is going to be some acrimony and I am sad if my going causes it.

Still plenty of time before July for peace to return.

Wednesday 7th February 1996

Puffs of white smoke from the study at around 2.30 pm to indicate decisions had been made. H—— and N—— have been successful while P—— and E—— are disappointed. The former seems quite happily resigned while the latter is looking dour. The appointments and aftermath took the whole day from 8.30 am to my coming in from bus duty at 3.30 pm for 45 minutes debriefing. I do hope N—— as an incomer – only 1½ terms with us – is given support and is not ostracised by those who feel longer servers should have been rewarded. He should bring in the necessary breath of fresh air.

The result of all this activity was that I was very much in charge on a day when fresh snow fell. [The snow] meant that pupils were again very high and the interviews meant bringing in a large number of supply staff. It was that feeling again of running faster and faster to keep pace. I have even had to bring routine marking home, something I try to avoid these days.

Taught a good Latin lesson to Year 8 and then went not properly prepared to Year 9. I let the lesson unfold but felt slightly uneasy and not being certain which direction it would take, a strange feeling for someone of my experience. I wonder if the pupils noticed or felt the uncertainty. I suspect not.

A very busy lunchtime with so much lively behaviour, euphemistically speaking, going on. Oh, for summer days when they can lounge on the grass!

The 1.35 pm bell meant final preparations for taking Full Assembly. Satisfying but draining.

Then to the ITT students: some are struggling and find our pupils difficult and cheeky. This is upsetting but I know it's often true.

Big Tree saga continues. More tomorrow.

Thursday 8th February 1996

BIG TREE has dominated today in many ways. Last night I was given the name of an arboriculturist in Bradford by Allan Dobson. I rang this gentleman this morning and after a little persuasion (initially £100 fee for coming out and report) he agreed to come on Saturday morning for a preliminary view; any discussion of fee would follow. By 12.00 noon he had rung to say he was coming this afternoon. On the phone he sounded a delightfully cheerful fellow.

I spent some time with Clive this morning discussing yesterday's appointments and their implications. I think he's beginning to realise he's going to have to adopt a more aggressive and dictatorial line with teaching colleagues, especially those who are failing. It is sad to say that there are teachers who are incompetent and we have had our fair share. They take up an undue proportion of senior managers' time and their pupils do not have a fair deal. In one case it may well be that parent power has a major influence in removing a colleague.

Raced through piles of marking and still found time to visit ITT students who seem to be coping quite well. A conversation with C—— revealed that he is very upset at my going and strongly believes that an attempt should have been made to replace me. Clearly N—— with only 1½ terms at KJS, as I said yesterday, is going to have a real battle to win support.

The tree man arrived at 4.00 pm. I carefully avoided our Bursar in the corridor who must be aware that attempts are being made to undermine her 'chop it down' philosophy. The arboriculturist, Mr Skeratt, was as pleasant as expected. It was clear he was amazed that a decision had been made to cut it down. To his expert eye there was no reason so to do; some judicious lopping here and there should see it standing for many more years. He will contact the Huddersfield Borough forester and agree a plan to save it. Full leaf in June should make it clearer what has to be done. Big Tree is mentioned in the school history in 1859 and seems safe for a few more years.

Heavy snow and high winds forecast for tomorrow. Let's hope Big Tree can stand the storm.

Friday 9th February 1996

092 DAYS TO GO

LAST night's forecast proved inaccurate but another storm was soon brewing. This was the day when pupil W——, known as 'Stone-the-Squirrels' for his past attempts to do so, set fire to supply teacher M——'s hair as he was standing behind her while waiting to enter a classroom. The event was tragi-comic, with more, I suppose, of the former than the latter. Of all the people to choose M—— was the last person pupil W—— should have chosen for his attempts to render a teacher a Joan of Arc. Her intense manner and un-yielding discipline encourage a naughty smile from me and I suspect from a few others. Nevertheless, he had to go and his father's girlfriend withdrew him at lunchtime. Clive was nearly in tears, for he had put so much time and effort in trying to 'save' him. His home background was so inadequate that he has to have sympathy although colleagues would like to have seen him moved on a year ago. But where to now? Almondbury High School? A fresh start? Sadly one sees him inside in a few years' time and someone has failed very badly.

News of my mother's unwillingness to go into a home despite her de-teriorating condition both mental and physical preyed on my mind and I felt down at the beginning of the day and unprepared for Year 9 Classical Studies. However, as is often the case, once into the room and the lesson, the mood changed and the teachers' equivalent of Doctor Footlights took over. Year 11 followed in a similar vein.

Much marking covered in a short time. Lunchtime saw some singing but rather short.

Two or three rather serious disciplinary incidents. Colleagues again see discipline breaking down. Is this true? February is a low time in the year and with one week to half term patience is at a very low ebb. Much staff absence today reflects the mood. Those with less stamina must be very tempted to have a day off.

My afternoon taken up by visit to the ITT students, and then when a record early buses departure looked likely one went off leaving most pupils behind. A telephone call, radio contact and it had to return even-tually.

Monday 12th February 1996

LAST Monday before a break. A typical teacher's approach to the beginning of a week in that it is common practice to see the year broken up into six blocks of half terms with the occasional extra day off which eases the pressure. Non-teachers no doubt think that this is a dreadful mentality. A cartoon over the weekend made the point when, prompted by the report of 15,000 incompetent teachers having a serious effect on pupils' education, elicited the comment, "It's a good job they have long holidays".

A very busy day indeed. As I said to Margaret yesterday evening after a run and a very tasty evening meal, "I feel so well but by tomorrow teatime I shall have that post-Monday feeling." Shall I have that Sunday night feeling constantly on retirement? I do hope so, for today by break (ie at 11.00 am) I had that tight-under-the-ribs feeling yet again which is brought on by pressure though I must say I have had it much less frequently over these last two or three years.

The morning was one of bits and pieces, all of which I felt I dealt with competently and none of which was major. However, they were so numerous and in some cases arriving concurrently that I felt I was being swamped at times. A secretary to help to filter out minor from major would have helped but that will never come in teaching.

Clive was very edgy about tonight's staff meeting which seemed likely to see him under pressure about school discipline.

Oldgate House wants pupil W—— ('Stone the Squirrels'[1]) – reinstated after 15 days but I'm sure the staff would revolt if that were to happen. My main disciplinary problem today was with the Year 11 pupil who simply loses control, knows he does and then very much regrets it. I am certain he is genuine and not spinning a tale.

As it turned out the staff meeting was non-controversial. Clive went down to town to lobby the LEA regarding the school budget which meant I took the last 20 minutes of the meeting. A smooth finish to a hectic day.

[1] *9th February 1996*

Tuesday 13th February 1996

I WONDER if the 13th was unlucky for our drama ITT student from Bretton? In many ways, he has dominated my thinking and consequent mood. I was aware he was struggling and in B——'s absence was having to take on more responsibility but this is his second practice. He asked to see me urgently but as I was teaching lessons 1 to 4 it had to be 11.20 am before that was possible. The man is ill with worry and insomnia but was highly critical of our pupils whom he described as being cheeky, rude and inattentive. He also declared the staff to be unsupportive; presumably I am included.

His tutor rang and will be in tomorrow morning. He has high regard for KJS so we'll see. Negative attitudes feed and produce more negative attitudes. Then I wonder if my impending departure is spreading unease and disquiet already; Margaret thinks this is the case.

I promised I would watch his lesson with Year 7 this afternoon. They are a lively class which he wound up with 25 minutes of playing party games. By the time I couldn't stand it any longer they were flying higher than the proverbial kites. At the end he said that those 25 minutes were the best he had had. After I left, he declared that their behaviour had deteriorated. My own Year 9 Latin lesson was excellent. He should have observed it. I know they are top sets but...

During the lesson I couldn't open the window. The temperature in the room was nearly tropical. At break I learned that our Bursar had told the caretaker to secure all windows as pupils had been seen sitting on windowsills and "might fall out". Clive ordered their immediate undoing.

A lunchtime sing was a pleasant 15 minutes' relief. There seems likely to be a 3% budget cut next year which sows more seeds of worry among staff already suffering from February Fatigue.

Wednesday 14th February 1996

IF Monday was up and Tuesday down then Wednesday was somewhere in the middle, perhaps shading to the positive rather than the negative.

The day's main issue was again the problems surrounding the Drama student [teacher]. Tony Chisholm from Bretton Training College was here by 8.50 am although he arrived when a myriad of other happenings was crowding in on me. I had to drop all and talk to him as I had a lesson some 25 minutes later. He was complimentary and very reassuring about the school's [role] and my role in particular – very uplifting after yesterday.

I'm sure most of the problems are of the student's own making. Will he ever make a teacher? Our combined fear is that he is very near the edge and our last wish is to tip him off or cause him to jump. The problems remain and I am not sure how they will be resolved. He must have taken up another 1½ hours of my time today.

Rang the bus company regarding the late K.78 and they expressed surprise at its repeated late arrival. Is there no check kept on such matters?

Lunchtime saw no break as I spent the entire time with Clive in his study debriefing on our Year 8 monitoring. Very informative but I still worry that so much input may lead to comparatively little output. We need stronger, more positive action in certain areas – or is this just me becoming cynical in my old age?

Best session with ITT students yet as we discussed day-to-day events and I conducted my favourite seminar on the marking and return of books.

Out to buses. The K.78 was late yet again. Kept back one Year 11 pupil who had been very rude to L—— and rang his mother immediately. She was supportive fortunately.

Twenty minutes' pleasant unwind in the staffroom and felt so much better.

Thursday 15th February 1996

QUITE a day. Taught only one lesson but hardly had a moment to reflect on what I should do next. Telephone calls, knocks at the door came so thick and fast that I again had that feeling of being swept along, not knowing which way to turn.

What a contrast, I presume, retirement will be. Too great a one? I feel somewhat apprehensive about this at times.

Yet my problems are minor compared with Clive's. He looks very worn and drawn. He has the ongoing disciplinary action concerning A——, M——'s incompetence through ill health, awkward parents again raising the question of the organisation of GCSE Science (ie by a single subject or by the Double Science award) and, above all, the proposed budget cuts of 3% which the Bursar declares could mean three or four fewer members of staff.

There had to be an emergency meeting of the three of us at 8.45 am, delayed by 10 minutes as a girl who had been barred [from school] today had been brought in by her father. She spent the day in isolation. How are we – sorry, 'they' – going to manage with even fewer members of staff, I cannot imagine.

I had to do some quick timetable calculations in spare moments and produce figures by 3.30 pm. One student [teacher] in tears because she couldn't cope with her first year pupils. She is very good but the little so-and-sos are ill disciplined, rowdy and simply not used to listening.

I taught a Year 8 lesson with the PE student [teacher] sitting in. It brought out the theatrical in me; he seemed genuinely impressed. There were numerous sendings out and sendings to me so I built my lower school assembly round the theme of 'improving behaviour'.

Played God, or at least Solomon, at 3.00 pm when a Year 11 pupil, an excellent student with an unblemished school record, was sent to me for having written three obscene lines – well written, I should add. He expected them to be sent to his parents. I simply said, as I tore them up and dropped them into the bin: "Always be careful when you put pen to paper." I am sure he will never forget this moment and he will learn from it.

A handshake and he left white-faced but no doubt greatly relieved.

Friday 16th February 1996

A GREAT feeling of relief sweeping over me as a break is coming up which, although it may bring the problem of persuading – if not forcing – my mother into a nursing home, will at least bring some respite from the pressures at KJS.

I feel at the moment that all-too-familiar queasiness which I have experienced so frequently at the end of the term or half term. Yet deep down I sense that both physically and mentally I'm not so low and after two or three days I'll be feeling fit enough to rejoin the human race in a satisfactory state of mind and body.

I was not particularly looking forward to today after the rigours of yesterday's depressing day. It left me with such a headache that, after defeating Peter Griffin 15-13 at singles badminton, the pain became increasingly bad – so much so that I had to cut short the session.

This morning's two double lessons went well, despite needing to gird up my mental loins. After that, it was a succession of telephone calls, visits, Presentation Evening preparations, snatched lunch and then a call-out to 'intruders'. These turned out to be our own Year 11s: six smokers on the perimeter of our school grounds. They were open and honest – disarmingly so. They did appear as young men, probably hooked already, and they have to be treated as such. I advised them that if they must smoke they must do so completely out of sight, especially of younger pupils.

News about Big Tree. A phone call from the Bradford arboriculturist revealed that his Huddersfield equivalent had also said that we should wait until full leaf in June. This confirms my suspicions that our Bursar continues to exceed her brief. She worries me and I wonder who will rein her in next year.

The half term finished with a debriefing session with Clive and Pat and then a few minutes of light-hearted banter in the staffroom. How I shall miss that atmosphere!

HALF-TERM BREAK

Monday 26th February 1996

IF asked "What have you done today to earn your brass?" I should have to consider very carefully before answering. I am aware that I have been so busy that by 11.00 am – beginning of break which wasn't – I had that pressure pain, as I sometimes term it, which has not been so unwelcomely apparent this year. I suppose it's partly because of the contrast between the last few days and [being] back in school.

Certainly the holiday was a most welcome one and I felt much better for it. However, it is difficult at times to separate home from school life and inevitably in unguarded moments thoughts of domestic bliss or difficulties creep in. The pleasure of seeing grandson, Jordi and family was offset by a mental picture of Margaret's mother now looking so frail and my own [mother] now in a home permanently, I hope for her sake. The attendant bitterness between my brother and sister-in-law and my mother's three sisters is causing distress.

Such thoughts were pushed to the back of my mind most of the time as I ploughed through post, took phone calls, answered knocks on the door and saw our moaning "had a rotten half term" drama student. I met for the first time the tutor from Huddersfield University in charge of Science.

I say again that a part-time secretary at least would make an enormous difference. The post did contain some interesting items, one from Australia and a very complimentary and moving letter from Trevor Carter, Old Almondburian and former footballing colleague. It's gone into my 'retirement correspondence' file.

Presentation Evening, of course, is uppermost in my mind and it will take up much of my time. I think we should celebrate on 6th March when it's over.

Management meeting from 2.00 until 4.15 pm. A very full agenda. Much planning for '96–'97 caused largely by my going. Shall I want to know the outcome?

Tuesday 27th February 1996

A VERY similar day to yesterday in so many ways. However, as I write this at 5.30 pm, the sun has just gone down below the horizon but has left a cheering orange-yellow glow. A visit to the greenhouse five minutes ago brought delight to the nostrils as they drank in that very particular, warm, earthy odour.

What has all this to do with school? Personally, it lifts the spirits enormously as it promises more time through lighter nights to indulge in horticultural delights and reminds me of the rapid passage of this final year. I do feel more mentally prepared to accept the Challenge of Change. So, despite another very hectic day and an early awakening – just before 5.00 am – I feel more relaxed.

Spoke about the importance of Presentation Evening in Briefing and hurried off to a Year 9 Latin class. I nearly committed a real *faux pas* when one of our few Asian pupils yawned loudly with mouth uncovered. My usual comment at such moments is "Was that an impersonation of (a) Wookey Hole, (b) Cheddar Gorge or (c) The Black Hole of Calcutta? I was beginning with (c) when I realised it was probably highly inappropriate.

Year 11 Latin, a lively start with this lovely, lively group, were doing a past paper under exam conditions. The technician had duplicated incorrectly and I had not checked. Such an embarrassing hiccup at the start of the lesson. Never a rest, and then through to 4.15 pm. No break, no lunch time apart from 15 minutes sing with M—— and Jack.

Worked with Head Girl on her speech and we are nearer getting an organist via Huddersfield University for the school song next Tuesday.

Took an assembly, met with C—— and L—— regarding the timetable for '96/'97.

We discovered that Year 9 truants yesterday had gone to the family planning clinic at the age of 13 to 14. Quite a change from the days of the Boys' Grammar School.

Wednesday 28th February 1996

I'M very tired again tonight. I walked home through the spring sunshine, birds a-twittering but felt very weary and this only the third day after a break. A brandy in coffee and a shower revived me somewhat but there's still GCSE marking and Presentation Evening preparation ...and the *Daily Telegraph* crossword if time permits.

The day began at 8.10 am with our Chairman of Governors, our Head of Music and I discussing Presentation Evening format. The chairman is really out of touch and his suggestions for 1960s musicals and songs from the time when I came to King James's was so embarrassingly inappropriate that we cringed (but I hope invisibly). Managed to dissuade him that 'the programme is already fixed' and there is 'no time to rehearse'.

Then there followed the predictable succession of knocks on door, phone calls and visits. It was a relief to go off to Year 8 Latin followed by Year 9 Classical Studies. The latter was hard work initially and for a set three they show remarkable ignorance of Time. But then, is it not my fault if they still have no concept of when Aristophanes was writing 'Peace'?[1]

Many matters came my way as Pat and Clive continue the Great Toilet Graffiti Investigation. The caretakers had painted the girls' toilets over the holidays which took up most of their time. By Tuesday all the walls were covered in indelible scrawl. It took Clive and Pat most of yesterday and today before three Year 9 girls eventually confessed. The result was six days' suspension and a bill for the caretakers' overtime, which will be large.

'Stone-the-Squirrels'[2] was on the premises at lunchtime. I thought he would be back. Rang his new school.

Excellent ¾ of an hour with our ITT students. Even the Drama one is improving but I don't really see him ever making a teacher.

A long phone call with Huddersfield Town Hall, short sing but was really too tired. Discussions with Clive and was excused tonight's Year 7 parents' meeting.

[1]*Athenian comedy written and produced by the Greek playwright Aristophanes, staged in 421 BC*

[2]*9th February 1996 and 12th February 1996. He had not been reinstated at KJS but was sent to another local school.*

Thursday 29th February 1996

083 DAYS TO GO

A DAY of much less pressure and continuing spring sunshine. The vernal awakening, lighter evenings, and warmer temperatures serve as a reminder that the year is slipping by very rapidly and tomorrow [will be] March already. House to sell and house to buy, such major undertakings, yet I am so bound up in the minutiae of everyday life at school.

Another colleague has had his car stolen – that's now three (or is it four?) since Christmas. That's one tenth of the staff. Such worries when the job is tough enough already. Had to do everyone's nightmare cover:

Period 2 Drama. Why do they spend so much time rolling on the floor, shouting and fighting? I could never teach drama. Eight periods like that would finish me off.

Enjoyed Year 8 Latin. It's only 30 minutes and it flies very rapidly but very satisfying. I rarely think 'this is the last time I'll cover the story' which I've probably done 20 times now. Is there a lurking feeling, nay hope, I may one day cover it again somewhere in some capacity?

Did some very routine work between 11.30 am and 12.30 pm sorting out prizes. Clive found me at it and we both agreed it was very sanity-restoring to spend some time on routine tasks.

Early lunch and then had a group of pupils helping to clean cups and paste plates in books ready for Presentation Evening. Made me realise how satisfying this informal relationship can be. It reminds me of scouting days when one wet week at camp built better relationships than forty in the classroom.

Clive suspended a pupil for 14 days for punching another in the eye, his second offence in two weeks but that's a long time. Is he deliberately cultivating a tougher image?

Today's smile. I sent two pupils to the caretaker to fetch cleaning material for cups. They came back with washing up liquid. The caretaker thought they were cleaning teacups not trophies.

CHAPTER 7

March
1996

– Presentation Evening –

Friday 1st March 1996

A SLIGHT headache which came on late afternoon lingers, the legacy of a demanding day at the end of a demanding week. Even more so for Clive who has had a succession of disciplinary matters with which to deal.

I sensed that this was depressing him so, despite his being very busy, I insisted on taking him up to the music room from which I had just returned. There, I had spent 10 minutes listening to the band/orchestra rehearsing for Tuesday's Presentation Evening. The sound that such groups produce still, literally, sends a shiver up my spine (or is it down?) and almost brings me to tears of joy. I made Clive listen for five minutes to remind him of the positive side of KJS and to remember that the large majority of our pupils are pleasant and well behaved. They are fortunate in having a superb music teacher who inspires them and thereby gives the school an excellent opportunity for some positive PR.

Weary this morning but Year 9 bottom set always gets me going. They are so naively keen although one or two show very clever insight and are sadly held back by their problems with English.

Year 11 Latin was a return of past papers which is so important, yet three were missing for an art exam[1]. How annoying when so much time has been put into marking. In Year 11, with some (both boys and girls), there seems to be an increasing problem as they are so near to leaving. They are also so worldly-wise and experienced that school and its restrictions must seem very hard to bear especially for those who are not going on to further education.

Frequent clashes with our LTAs meant too many were sent to me. 20 minutes' escape at lunchtime when the four of us sang the best for a long time.

[Went] over the Head Girl's speech again, then off to cover A——'s lesson. He is on a disciplinary hearing at Oldgate House. Finished up teaching the lesson as it speeded up the passage of time.

[1] *With the proliferation of examinations, such subjects such as Art with its practicals and Languages with its orals tended to spread well outside the normal examination times. On this occasion three of DAB's Latin students had to take their first Art practicals at a time when he was returning important Latin papers.*

Monday 4th March 1996

ONE hundred and eleven days gone. In cricket the score at this point is known as a 'Nelson'[1] and suggests something unlucky is about to happen. It's not been a particularly satisfying day although it could have been tomorrow and I desperately want that to be one of good omen. I suppose the importance and the finality of tomorrow are preying on my mind and I constantly think 'roll on Wednesday morning' although I know that Wednesday will see Clive and Pat out all day. This will almost certainly mean it will be onerous.

What has concerned me today in particular have been the disciplinary problems. This makes me worry immodestly [about] what things will be like next year when I've gone, and the year after that when Jack has retired at the age of 65 after 38 years here. Schools reflect society and are a microcosm of the same; so with the breakdown of the family, the decline in respect for law, order and the elderly and the mushrooming drug culture, it's hardly surprising that these changes bring their attendant problems into schools.

Today a teacher lost control of a class and sent out seven pupils, a boy produced a lighter which he used to singe another boy's coat after waving it in front of his face. Pat confirms that girls have brought drugs into school and have smoked cannabis on site. And ours is a 'good school' and the wonderful things which will be said about it tomorrow night will make me feel proud, somewhat concerned and no doubt relieved that next year it won't be my responsibility.

Despite all, I do still feel optimistic and have to remind myself that those causing problems are in a very small minority and the vast majority of our pupils are delightful and need and deserve our care. It is the fault of society at large, not theirs.

Half an hour on the telephone this evening to Andrew Taylor planning tomorrow night's procedures.

[1] *The cricket score of 111 is called a 'Nelson' after Admiral Nelson, who supposedly only had one eye, one arm and one leg near the end of his life. Cricket-lovers with a better awareness of history know that Nelson never in fact lost a leg and prefer to say 'one eye, one arm and one ambition'.*

Tuesday 5th March 1996

IT'S Presentation Evening at Huddersfield Town Hall. Having partaken of an excessive amount of mayoral whisky in the mayor's parlour after proceedings I was in no state to complete writing up this entry until the following day. This, I suppose, is an exaggeration for I was not inebriated; but a combination of the hard stuff, plus elation, plus exhaustion and plus an inevitable partial sense of anti-climax meant that, despite not going to bed until after midnight, I was awake very early to reflect on a very significant and memorable day.

I was up again by 4.00 am and as I write this in the colder, sober light of Wednesday morning I can now reflect more objectively on my last Presentation Evening, formerly known as Speech Day. Initial reactions or reflections? Inevitably one of great relief. My voice did not give out, I did not break down but was most self-conscious of a trickling tear at one moment – was it seen? [Just] as students emerging from an exam frequently think only of all the bits that they got wrong, so I needle myself with thoughts of the wrong name read out near the end, a stumble over a title, and planting kisses on the cheeks of lady friends at the end of the session in the parlour – including the deputy mayoress. How improper! Did she mind?

The morning practice went well, much better than last year. My annual jokes were ready to be trotted out. "Do not go to the toilets unless absolutely necessary. Last year a Year 7 pupil went and was lost in the bowels of the town hall for three days". Then, "It is not unusual for those massive chandeliers above us to tremble during the singing of the school song". I looked up and they were not there – the first time in 35 years. Improvising quickly, I said that they must have been taken down for health and safety reasons just in case they fell.

The evening did go very well, I must agree. It's all so familiar to me but to the less experienced apparently it was all very impressive. The Head Girl's speech was superb. Old Almondburian Andrew Taylor, speech-deliverer and prize-presenter, was excellent. Clive and others said very kind words about me and the Father Willis organ[1] thundered out 'Floreat Schola'.

Then I heard that my beloved Lincoln City had won 3-2 at Scunthorpe. Icing on a very tasty cake.

[1] *The Father Willis organ was originally built in 1860 for an exhibition hall in Newport, South Wales and was bought for the new Huddersfield Town Hall in 1881.*

Wednesday 6th March 1996

AND so back down to earth, back to reality or return to the grindstone – whichever cliché one may care to choose. Clive and Pat were out all day preparing themselves for Ofsted next autumn [by which time] I shall be swanning off to or sunning myself in pastures new.

I was due to take full assembly, meet five staff from Greenhead Sixth Form College coming to interview Year 11 students, do bus duty, hold an ITT students' seminar, teach three lessons, greet Bretton tutor coming to appraise his four students and any other events which the day would surely throw up; all these happenings, fixed or unpredictable, passed through my mind on the 18 or 19 minute walk to King James's.

As the sun, appropriately, was shining this morning my step was lighter and so was the day, much more so than anticipated. In fact it passed quickly and pleasurably. I did cut it short by coming home soon after 3.30 pm as I felt positively sleepy by then.

The lessons went really well; one can tell when the pupils or students – I have difficulty viewing our Year 11s as 'pupils' – are enjoying a lesson and that's still a very satisfying thrill after 35 years. Enjoyed also a little seminar with three bright Year 11 Latin students who had been doing an Art GCSE exam when the last GCSE Latin 'unseen' was returned.

I then hurried off to an assembly of the whole school. "Thank you, thank you very much," I began. "Thank you all those who attended for making my last Presentation Evening so emotionally memorable." I feel they were quite touched. I mentioned in particular the songs sung by Key Stage 3 (Years 7, 8 and 9) and what a lovely sight and sound it had been.

A few disciplinary problems to sort out but all comparatively minor and then there was news that the school is to receive a £10,000 grant to establish Internet links with Scotland and Ireland. I shall not be there but I'm still delighted.

Thursday 7th March 1996

IF yesterday was comparatively calm and easy, then today has has been hectic verging on the hellish. Clive was off again today taking his son to his third university interview.

I am going to list the incidents in preparation for relating some to him tomorrow. We had five All Saints[1] pupils on the premises at lunchtime who were very reluctant to leave. Three boys in the toilets during assembly, one for a second time in three days. One Year 9 thumped another who stormed off the premises, slamming doors and kicking crates around. One new boy was out of L——'s lesson after crawling around on the floor. He admits the same but has no explanation. The police were in regarding pupil R—— who again has run off. According to the police he is living in a tent with a girl in the Shepley area. One new girl skipped PE with two others, lay on the seats in the bus bay and lit a small fire nearby. Four Year 11s set about another girl 'just for fun'. I sent two of them home immediately as they have already been suspended four or five times for similar behaviour. There may be other incidents but things happen so thick and fast it was difficult at times to cope.

If I read this in one year's time, I do hope I can be reminded how tense I felt by 3.15 pm [with] that tight feeling yet again; then I can contrast it with the relaxed state I shall be in. Occasionally I feel guilty to be leaving at such demanding times, but then I salve my conscience by telling myself, "You've done your best for 35 years, not taken time off and rarely looked the other way. You deserve your retirement." If I say this often enough then perhaps that guilt-ridden feeling of walking out will go away.

I did teach a Year 8 Latin group but felt impatient and grumpy which is abnormal. I also had 10 minutes' singing at lunchtime but felt so weary and yawned frequently that I did not perform well. In between

I marked two sets of books but these too rather spasmodically i.e. not straight through. Predictably pupils had not done well. Their fault or mine?

[1]*All Saints College, Bradley Bar, Huddersfield; about 5 miles from King James's School*

Friday 8th March 1996

AND so another day passes, another week completed and – whatever the mood – that boundless creature called Time marches on relentlessly, with 23 weeks of the teaching year gone already. On occasions, I do feel very consciously picked up, carried along and plonked down at the end of the week, especially one so demanding physically, mentally and emotionally as in the one now passed.

I was ready to tell Clive that I really felt things are on the slide and was prepared to list the causes of my 'disgruntlement' but in the end I backed away because (a) what's the point in upsetting him when his burden is heavy enough already; (b) causing dissension at this advanced stage of the year; (c) when, after a reasonable night's sleep, I felt less unhappy this morning and (d) who is to say I am right and he, who seems so much less concerned about disciplinary matters, is wrong?

Certainly staff are very ready to moan and certain ex-staff, now 'on supply' are up in arms about not being treated as they were when they were full time. That's bound to be the case and I've no doubt I would have similar challenges should I ever do supply elsewhere.

I wasn't particularly looking forward to teaching this morning. We are at the end of the week and I was suffering from self-imposed post-badminton fatigue. As is often the case, the lessons went very well. What a contrast between consecutive teaching groups. Year 9 bottom set Classical Studies are a lovely little group, and reading *Peace*[1] with them again convinced me that despite difficulties there are some lively, receptive minds there.

Then to Year 11 Latin with an ITT student observing. They put on an excellent show. Fifteen minutes' escape to the music practice room and a great sound produced. When shall we record our first disc? Only joking.

Just as I was leaving an angry parent rang to say how eggs, flour and talcum powder had been thrown around on the K.83 [bus], ostensibly celebrating someone's birthday. Monday morning's first task will be to investigate.

[1]*Aristophanes: see 28th February 1996*

Monday 11th March 1996

THE K.83 saga took up a considerable amount of time today. The situation is worse than first impressions. A Year 11 'trusty' whose grandparent rang with further information but also feared for her granddaughter's safety (I have no great fear as she is tall and very hefty) revealed that eggs and flour had been stolen from the Home Economics store. Similar things had happened also on the previous evening. Secondly the bus windows and seats were in a dreadful state. I rang the bus company who were already aware of the situation as the bus had been inspected on Friday, post-journey, so we must await developments. I hope the offenders can be faced with a substantial bill and banned from using buses. We shall see, as the bus company has previously been reluctant to take strong action.

I felt somewhat lethargic after an enjoyable weekend when son Alan had been up to stay. It had been most enjoyable and I saw it as a taste of more next year when we shall be able to 'spend more time with the family'.

Clive was out in court all day representing the school in a claim against it. Somebody had injured an ankle on an insecure or broken manhole cover in the school grounds. The fact she should not have been there in the first place is apparently irrelevant. He left at 10.00 am and had not returned by 4.00 pm. What a waste of his and our precious time! I tried to suggest to him before he went that he needs to manage his time better, to be a little less conscientious and fastidious; but I suspect he'll never change. Or perhaps it was a little presumptuous of me but I do have his interests at heart.

Inevitably, his absence placed a greater burden on those left behind. I took a Year 11 assembly and rampaged over the bus incident but still said how much I enjoyed talking and meeting our older pupils as they mature and generally act like young responsible adults.

Chaired a management meeting in Clive's absence and felt bold enough to make strong suggestions regarding next year. It would be easier to say little but I can't bring myself to do that.

Tuesday 12th March 1996

THE bus saga continues in that I've made contact with the person in charge of such matters at the bus company. She confirms that the bus had to be taken out of service for cleaning and that she is prepared to send a bill and also ban the main offenders from using the buses for a period of days. I suspect there will be resistance from parents knowing the situation and the home backgrounds.

The day began with a lively and rewarding Year 9 Latin class and then Year 11 Latin doing their first revision paper. Marked it on and off during the day. For the most part 'sound' to 'very good' but three were very weak and one dreadfully so. I desperately want them all to gain at least a grade C or above in my last public exam group but the weak ones need to work much harder and/or be inspired in the belief that they can 'pass'. This does usually happen, but at this stage I often wonder how they can improve sufficiently before exam day.

Had five minutes' notice at break that L—— had gone home ill. When I saw it was a Year 8 bottom set next for her – and knowing her problems – I suspect the prospect of an hour and ten minutes with them exacerbated her condition. Definitely a failing teacher but will she be encouraged out?

Complaints too from some top set girls in M——'s group. Here is another one who has struggled for 20 years but is still with us. If only the profession would grasp the nettle. It would be so much easier for all and a better education for pupils. However, the problem remains of finding teachers sufficiently qualified and able to teach shortage subjects. I genuinely believe that our present ITT students are sound but the weaker one (i.e. the borderline case) will still pass. I presume they will all get jobs eventually somewhere.

Interviewed three Year 11 girls in our 'encourage-them-to-get-5Cs' campaign. Assurances were given – and then one skipped English five minutes later.

Wednesday 13th March 1996

THE 13th. A cold day both literally and metaphorically. Winter has re-established its icy grip. Some snow, much ice, pupils indoors, no PE outside, no unwinding in warm spring sunshine. All this seems to bring a feeling of restriction and tenseness among both teachers and taught.

It did not, however, prevent five Year 9s skipping lessons 3 and 4 to spend the time near the cricket pavilion. What did they have, what did they do to keep them – three boys and two girls – warm in that biting wind? Each other? From my lofty equine seat I took it as a personal affront that the two girls preferred that retreat to my Classical Studies lesson. Added to the offence was the initial deceit and [the fact that] they had been in serious disciplinary trouble one week ago ; and they knew I'd find out and that I would inform their parents. And still they went ahead.

They missed a good lesson. Sophocles' *Oedipus* always grips them. I suppose it is the incestuous, murderous, bloody plot that appeals but it is still great to see them gripped by it[1]. I was also moved by that 'magic moment' when I put the word 'circumspectaverunt' on the board and asked those bright eyed Year 8s to imagine they were to explain it to their parents; how to break the work down to elicit its meaning. They worked at it in pairs, pointing regularly to the board, discussing, arguing, giving me, after 35 years, a warm feeling deep down. What ultimate use was the challenge? Why do we have to justify everything in terms of 'use'? It was, I believe, a valuable joint exercise.

The bus saga rumbles on. One of the main protagonists is in trouble for striking another pupil. There are serious domestic difficulties here. She said "I know there's a good girl inside wanting to get out." Little

Miss Nose Stud arrived at my room with her book and I made her take the stud out. "My parents say I am not to." "And I say you have to." She did and I await the inevitable angry response.

Discussed the budget with ITT students and then talked with Clive and Pat until 4.15 pm on 'Sanctions'.

[1]*The Athenian tragedy by Sophocles was first performed around 429 BC. Its grisly plot ends with Oedipus, King of Thebes, gouging out his own eyes in despair.*

Thursday 14th March 1996

Anything, in school or schools in general, is rendered completely insignificant in the light of yesterday's Dunblane Primary School massacre[1]. Our problems: a nose stud? A skipped lesson? And yet, as I said to the ITT students yesterday, 'The show must go on.'

Caught up in the hurly-burly of everyday life in a secondary school, secondary issues are pushed aside. An amazing phone call at 8.25 am. The girl who spent my lesson yesterday at the cricket pavilion had told her mother, "Mr Bush was wrong. I was in the sickbay and he has apologised." The mother was ringing to confirm this was true. So contrite was the girl that she skipped history, or most of it, but insisted she had [just] slipped out five minutes early. She is, according to my colleagues, in line for the 'Liar of the Year' award at next year's Presentation Evening. Mother and child booked in for a meeting tomorrow.

The expected phone call from Little Miss Nose Stud's parents never materialised. According to her form teacher the nose stud was in but taken out on her advice. So perhaps, little by little, we are getting there. There seem to have been numerous incidents today but with excellent assistance from others, especially W—— who seems to be taking on my mantle, I felt we coped well. Phone calls to parents generally brought support.

As I reminded colleagues, it is so very important to remember that the vast majority of our pupils are, like pupils in general, all very pleasant. They are a pleasure to be with, so responsive and yet so vulnerable.

Short chat with Clive about planning the budget. The day did end on a positive note with all the buses, even the K.78, away by 3.23 pm – a record.

[1]*The Dunblane School massacre took place at Dunblane Primary School near Stirling, Scotland on 13th March 1996 when Thomas Hamilton shot 16 children and one teacher dead, injured 15 others and then killed himself. It remains the deadliest mass shooting in British history.*

Friday 15th March 1996

GOOD heavens, Friday again! It's been a wearying week and I've decided not to go to an inaugural PTA-type occasion tonight. Writing 'occasion' reminded me that this word spelt 'ocassion' had been written thus by a member of the English Department today, along with other similar errors.

My excuse for non-attendance this evening is simply tiredness. I've not felt 100% this week and even badminton last night was an effort. "If you can play badminton then you can't be that ill" says t'other half, not without some justification. That's true but I don't feel like turning out again tonight. However, I'm full of admiration for all those colleagues who will be there.

What dominated today? I suppose the staff who are angry, indeed very angry, about the sudden ban on their personal use of the office photocopier. A bureaucratic system has been set up by our Bursar to be implemented from Monday onwards. Indeed it will be highly inconvenient, "making a difficult job more difficult" as R—— put it. The Bursar has gone to Florence today for a long weekend and will be back next Tuesday. How indiscreet – and how unwise, in my opinion, of Clive to allow it. He's been away nearly all day at a Heads' conference of some kind. How cynical I'm sounding.

My Year 9 Classical Studies group was as delightfully simple as always. Year 11 Latin lesson fell apart halfway through when the 'Unseen under exam conditions' had the 1991 paper with a 1992 vocabulary. Good job I was not being observed. Had to abandon it and do it orally with 'Sir' acting as the vocabulary sheet. Up to Integrated Studies after break where

W—— was having the usual problems. I removed three boys. Five minutes later a phone call from him again. "Pupil R—— is listening to music on his CDROM!" Wouldn't – indeed couldn't – have happened in 1961. I phoned his parents and the result was an immediate after-school detention.

Some patrolling in the afternoon and I felt the week finished in a controlled way. Uproarious laughter in the staff room over the sex education packs[1], whereas the pupils take it all in their stride and very calmly. Not the slightest hint of a snigger. A perfect example of the generation gap.

[1] *The Education Act 1996 required that sex education should inform pupils about STIs (Sexually Transmitted Infections) and HIV (Human Immun-odeficiency Virus) and encourage pupils to have due regard to 'moral con-siderations and family life'. It became compulsory for schools to teach the bi-ological aspects of puberty, reproduction and the spread of viruses and infection.*

Monday 18th March 1996

WHY did I sense today, more than for some time, that I really am approaching the end? The dinner-ladies asking Jack to discover what I would like as a leaving present? The fact that I have fixed a meeting with the estate agent with a view to putting 8 Foxglove Road on the market in the very near future? That I felt myself taking a back seat in discussions on both academic and pastoral matters, [thereby] being gently and not involuntarily sidelined from fixing next year's Presentation Evening? A combination, I suppose.

Not a very busy day. I tried to avoid buzzing around corridors, "looking for trouble" as Margaret would say. I did find some by 9.00 am. L——, a failing teacher, had five pupils sent out already and they were on the loose. Returned them to the classroom but the school has a real problem there. Two ITT students are also not really coping. I felt like ringing their tutors as a matter of urgency but I know [the students] will in the end all pass, just as they all have in the past.

The first day of the new regime following the duplicating ban, while the Bursar is in Florence. Our staff are furious. It really is making a tough job tougher, as I suggested last week. Management meeting foreshortened for a pastoral at 3.15 pm but still I have this feeling that there is too much theorising and too little emphasis on the practical. Do I keep quiet? I've more or less decided I'll do no boat-rocking.

'Rock my cradle, not my boat', I've adopted as my motto.

Tuesday 19th March 1996

AS I write these lines, the thoughts uppermost in my mind revolve around house sales, vending boards, surveyors and solicitors. The estate agents have been and the first steps taken along the road to the south-west.

Yet I have to push all this to the back of my mind and think about school, the '96–'97 timetable, budgets and related matters. With a 2-3% cut in the money coming into the school for next year, planning is becoming critical and [it's all] very worrying for the colleagues I shall be leaving behind. There is a gradual realisation that even with my departure and that of B—— we (sorry, the school!) will almost certainly have to shed staff. For me: relief to be away from it all; for them: nagging uncertainty.

After a demanding Spanish class at the technical college [yesterday evening] followed by a sound night's sleep and a *Nytol*, I felt refreshed. However, Year 9 Latin, which should have been the highlight of the week, was a strangely subdued lesson; and I don't know why. It just did not seem to flow, despite my good-humoured encouragement. Year 11 Latin following was much more upbeat but it was sad to see our perky Head Girl looking very down at the end, knowing she had not done a very good test.

Our ponderous Drama student [teacher] is annoying me intensely. He says he did wish to teach initially, but seems already to avoid the classroom. He opted out of an activity today so that he could "do some work for his girlfriend on his computer".

Timetable planning with C——, L—— and Clive and [I have] that feeling of unreality again. I have planned timetables for so many years – and I'm now doing it with my own initials missing from the staff list.

Wednesday 20th March 1996

A BAD night and houses, pupils and associated problems pouring through my weary mind at 3.30 am. Yet despite that, a satisfactory and satisfying day in most ways.

Tonight it is Year 10 parents' evening. It's a year I don't teach and I had not intended attending but as Clive had forgotten about it – the man is human – and Pat wanted to avoid this one, I have agreed to look in which means an hour's stay at least.

I am conscious that I have recorded little of humour of late and yet most days there is some at some point. Let me mention two moments today, one white, one black. While studying *Cena (The Meal)*[1] with Year 8 Latin I trotted out my usual quip. "You can see these Romans having chicken and chips. No chips? Why not?" Answer: (a) because the Romans didn't have frying pans and (b) they had no oil in which to fry them!

During Year 9 Classical Studies I showed them a video of *Oedipus* – the final scene where he enters, eyes stabbed, blood pouring down his cheeks. I was informed later by her best friend M—— that poor S——, sitting only one yard from the screen, can't stand the sight of blood and sat for the last five minutes with her eyes firmly closed. How I felt for her, poor lass!

After break, a pupil whose father has been inside for violence, was in isolation. He had attacked another pupil and H—— was unable to separate them. T—— was called in and [although] a big man and the pupil relatively small it was only with great difficulty that he managed to restrain him and then remove him forcibly from the scene. Reddened arms were now on show and the pupil stating boldly that he was going to sue T——. Chances are that he'll change school. How will the father react?

I should have mentioned yesterday that little Miss Nose Stud is now Little Miss Red-Mark-on-the-Nose, i.e. it's gone during the school day.

Five undesirables were on the premises at lunchtime; this does cause hassle and anxiety. I telephoned the police and Almondbury High School. They are 'known'.

Very popular staff member, Miss W's birthday today. Do I call for "Happy Birthday, Miss W" tonight? Does my going allow such flippancy?
[1]*Pupils followed the Cambridge Latin Course originally introduced by former Latin teacher Jim Toomey*

Thursday 21st March 1996

IS it Pliny who in one passage, which must have been in a set book or 'unseen', asks at the end of the day what he has achieved and has difficulty answering his own question? Certainly, that is my problem today for it has been one hell of a day. By 4.00 pm I had a pressure headache, the direct result of rushing or being rushed from one phone call, problem or classroom visit to another. What a contrast retirement will be. Shall I be able to cope with it? And yet, if I try to think of one job or problem which ate up a major part of the day I have difficulty in selecting it. I had more than seven hours without any break – even lunch saw pupils and LTAs coming to the staff table. After not being home until 9.45 pm from Parents' Evening last night this meant inevitable tiredness this morning.

More bullying on the bus last night. The main culprit, a Year 8 girl with 'previous convictions', is a real thug already and I do use the word advisedly. Truanting today so I could tackle the mother on two fronts. Although I have no real power so to do, I have banned her from using the buses for six days. Another Year 10 pupil was attacked by six youths from Almondbury High School at lunchtime. What a violent world – and this is in a reasonably well-behaved part of town.

Year 8 Latin worry me. It's clear from their homework they are finding the concept, and therefore translation of tenses, very difficult, more so I feel than in previous years. Now is this the result of poor teaching or less able pupils? Jack and I were the subject of an interview by Clive's Year 9 English class. Enjoyable but it took 30 minutes out of the day. Trying to mark two sets of books while dealing with day-to-day problems and phone calls. Nevertheless, a magic five minutes with Jack when he and I did a double act in front of a gullible Year 7. Typical was asking "Is Yasser Arafat here?" A pupil replied "I think he is in Year 8, Sir" and he was not joking. I think.

Friday 22nd March 1996

On such a day as this I really am glad to be retiring. It's rare that I have felt so strongly both physically and mentally that I've had enough. Physically? By 1.30 pm I had that great pressure ache I call it, under the ribs.

Will July mean that I shall never experience that feeling again? Mentally? Depressing. Although the majority of our pupils do remain pleasant, cheerful and willing to listen and learn, there are increasing numbers, so it seems, who are rebellious, insolent and ill-disciplined and they make life so difficult, draining teachers of the energy and enthusiasm to do their job properly. As I saw one Year 9 youth sauntering truculently away from a colleague, I thought back to the early '60s when such behaviour, if it had occurred, would have meant a caning and unlikely repetition of such an attitude in the future. On Monday, he will be back doing the same again.

'Child-centred education' and 'pupils' rights'. "What rubbish!" says a so-long-in-the-tooth teacher. The pendulum will swing back, it always does. 'Teacher-centred' will become the norm again but it will take time. We've gone so far down the present road that I feel deeply for those entering the profession, if it is still regarded as one, for they face a daunting, uphill struggle. I could not advise anyone to enter the teaching profession today without warning them of the problems to be encountered.

Clive and a Year Head were both off, as were five ancillary staff. The result was [that] those senior staff remaining were bombarded with problems while trying to teach, mark and plan curriculum documents. Clive returned late in the afternoon. 'Do not disturb' on his door. I felt like disturbing him loudly. To what avail? To unburden myself? To complain? To spoil his weekend? In the end I did nothing. Nor did I take a call from an irate father. I had "gone home". Monday will be another day.

Let's open a bottle of Rioja red...

Monday 25th March 1996

IF only the weather would improve! Now I suppose that such outside agencies should not affect one's professional performance but inevitably for some it does. Is it a question of ions? In my case, it is simply that I'm fed up with day after day of sunless skies, low temperatures and drizzle.

Today at 4.00 pm, five days into spring, it is so foggy that visibility is down to 40 yards, car headlights are on and the temperature is 3.5° C. This after a meteorologically depressing weekend. [But it's] 15°C and sunny in the south. To warmer climes!

Consequently not feeling very buoyant as I trudged uphill to school along the muddy paths. I was still full of Friday. Clive arrived at my room at 10.00 am so I poured out my feelings about Friday's difficulties. He has a very nasty looking eye infection of some kind, probably brought on by stress, so I tried not to get too angry. He's having enough problems with our Bursar who is expecting an upgrade and yet most people seem to feel that her leaving the school would be generally very beneficial.

I found myself taking things easy this morning and feeling guilty for so doing. The problem pupils of Friday resurfaced, although one, with us in theory for three weeks, has moved on to Barnsley. Another, exceedingly economical with the truth, told Clive he had had no homework set and Clive believed him. Jack and M—— intervened to say that work had been set and that the pupil had refused to copy it down.

The management meeting lasted 2½ hours. Initially I was bored with the theorising but became enlivened when on to practical matters. That's me but I still believe there is too much of the first and too little of the second.

Tuesday 26th March 1996

TIME: 5.05 pm. Late home this evening although some in in industry would not think so. I have to be out again soon after 6.30 pm for a Year 8 Parents' Evening and I know it will be a very long session. I suspect it will be 9.30 pm before I'm home again, then wearily to bed taking the evening with me and, before I seem to have rolled over, I'll be back to school tomorrow morning. Still this is the penultimate Parents' Evening. There is Year 9 to come after Easter and then that's it.

Another very busy day. Marking began before school and after Briefing there began the handing over procedure, stage one. N—— should pick up my present Latin Year 9. I regret very much not being able to take them through to GCSE but I assured them that they'll be in excellent hands and sincerely hope that a viable group forms. In days of a very tight budget it would be very upsetting if the subject were to fold [at King James's] after, I suppose, approaching 400 years. Latin must have been taught at some stage ever since the school's 1608 foundation.

I left them after 15 minutes. N—— took over and I went off to his low-ability Classical Studies group to read *Peace* yet again but still enjoyable. To Year 11 Latin and more exam practice. Some excellent results. I have marked most already but a couple of very weak ones and one in particular. Is she going to spoil my 100% record?

Two OAS items today. I received a very moving letter from Gerald Hinchliffe, author of the school history[1] and a visit from Lawrence Crabtree[2] at lunchtime.

The most interesting development in the afternoon was the arrival of a copy of the staffroom committee minutes. It contained direct criticism of our Bursar, of management over discipline and a tirade against the new printing and duplicating system. Also I must remember that a hand on the shoulder of a pupil these days weakens one's disciplinary case. And to think what we got away with in the '60s.

But that was a dreadful era, was it not?

[1] *The late Gerald Hinchliffe (King James's Grammar School 1933-40) was the author of A History of King James's Grammar School in Almondbury, published in 1963*

[2] *A member of the Old Almondburians' Society, now resident in the USA, who attended King James's Grammar School from 1941-46*

Wednesday 27th March 1996

A SOLID night's sleep thanks to exhaustion and *Nytol*. One might ask if the latter was necessary but I do know that going to bed, even exhausted, and yet with mind stimulated by an event such as Parents' Evening does often mean restlessness.

Woke feeling semi-drugged but perked up on the way to school as, at last, the sun was shining and the skies were blue though it was still cold; and so it has remained all day. It does seem to have lifted everyone's spirits – pupils' and staff's. Last night had been rewarding but tiring. I can think of no other occasion when time passes so quickly. I talked to parents without a break from 6.40 to 9.25 pm. I did not look at my watch until the end. If asked the time, I would have guessed shortly after 8.00 pm.

Arrived in school expecting firecrackers but only heard damp squibs. The controversial minutes meant that Clive invited the staffroom committee to his room at 12.30 pm. I was invited but declined. Why? Partially because I have much sympathy with their complaints – but not with the mode of delivery – and particularly because I am easing out and I feel I should be letting next year's team ease in.

Year 8 Latin was excellent but Year 9 Classical Studies struggled because I had not really thought it through properly; I am sure they were unaware but I certainly was.

A busy lunchtime but managed 15 minutes' sing.

A mother rang to complain that I had grabbed hold of her daughter last Friday, spun her round causing her to bang her head and go home with a bump on the same. What an absolute lie! But how worrying. The mother declared it was just my word against hers. How vulnerable we are!

Covered for Pat [Reid] while she talked to the ITT students. This was a Year 8 Maths class, Set 2 and I was amazed to see them adding up – for example – 200+35 on their calculators.

Thursday 28th March 1996

TODAY seems to have been dominated by disciplinary matters. So much energy and time are expended in this field these days that one is tempted to ask if this is what schools are now really about.

In Briefing on post-Year 8 parents' meeting, various names of pupils were read out who were no longer to sit near each other as they were mutually distracting. As Jack said, "That problem has never arisen in my lessons" – and it never will, Jack. If one's discipline is firm and is ideally dosed liberally with humour – as his is – this problem will never arise.

By 8.35 am news of a window, frame and all, being out of girls' toilets and three Year 11 boys beating a hasty retreat was reported by Year 8 supergrass girls. When summoned, one denied everything but the second quickly cracked and within five minutes all three had admitted that they were in the girls' toilets and were unable to escape as B—— was patrolling outside. Therefore they had decided to escape via the window. The first took the frame and glass with him with noisily shattering results. A new meaning to 'you've been framed'!

My subsequent interviewing should have been videoed. I know that sounds awfully boastful but for direct, time-saving methods, I'm sure it could not have been bettered. There was no "Come in, sit down, let's talk this over".

Year 8 Latin: 'Felix the slave' was translated as 'cat' and the pupil was quite happy to write down 'The cat drained the wine cup.'

Later, a Year 9 pupil whom I knew had been in the bushes during assembly, denied it repeatedly. It has always amazed me how ingrained such a habit of lying becomes. She admitted it only when a fellow assembly-skipper told her to her face she was there.

Trouble is brewing for a supply CDT teacher who has manhandled one of our recently arrived Year 8 pupils, a real pest in the making. The pupil, that is, not the teacher.

Friday 29th March 1996

JUST realised that more than ⅔ of the academic year has gone. I must check if my countdown is correct. It would be embarrassing to find an odd day left over at the very end. As I sip a sherry and the sun still shines at 5.42 pm, I reflect that indeed the year slips so rapidly by.

An even more visually striking reminder this evening. As I turned into Foxglove Road I could immediately see an Eddison's [Estate Agent] 'For Sale' notice standing out brightly and boldly outside number 8. Although it was expected around now, its presence certainly produced what our children, Alan and Catherine, used to call a 'lurch' ie a slight churn of the stomach.

As for the school day, not bad at all. Is it the sunshine that's lifting spirits? Jack's humour always helps. He is such a valued colleague and a very dear friend to me. When a female games teacher burst unannounced into the room where he was changing, he declared he wished to protest. "But I didn't do anything, I didn't see anything", she retorted. "That's why I wish to protest!" he said. Typical Jack!

Badminton last night and a touch of a cold meant I woke feeling very weary this morning. [Perhaps] this is partially self- induced – too vigorous a sport at the age of 56+? But I did beat Jason W 15-2 at singles (such immodesty!) so I felt mentally uplifted. All this meant that getting going by 8.45 am was very hard.

The day began with a difficult lesson, a Set 6 CSD; my fault not theirs. I was aware of the lesson dragging and that's a very rare feeling for me. Fortunately, it picked up pace by the end and I wonder if they sensed it. Year 11 Latin was much better and I enjoyed the gentle banter with these very bright young adults, almost at the end of their secondary school life. Such moments are so precious. After the awful feeling I had last Friday today it was very peaceful.

Indeed by mid afternoon, the patrol-the-corridors time, the school was re-markably calm apart from one Maths student [teacher] who is struggling with Year 7. He is a pleasant fellow and he'll pass but I doubt if he will ever make a really effective teacher.

Yesterday's CDT supply teacher will complete his supply next week and then "We won't use him again" says Clive.

CHAPTER 8

April
1996

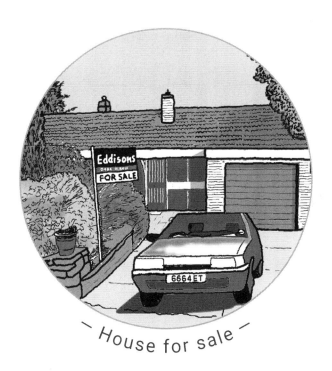

~ House for sale ~

Monday 1st April 1996

THE sun shone and I slipped home early. Surely not DAB becoming demob happy? No, I don't believe so although I did feel guilty. Despite the sun, it's still only 6° C and white all over this morning. Oh, for some southern European warmth! We are looking forward to taking holidays out of school time in warmer climes, more perhaps than anything else.

April Fools' Day: for the most part jokes were weak although the staff one "Go and ask Mr X for a long stand", keeping the pupil waiting and then sending him on to Mrs Y for the same was cruelly amusing. I sent B—— a note from the office to say that Chelsea had been re-instated in the FA Cup [semi-final] as Manchester United had played an ineligible player. (Yesterday Manchester United beat Chelsea 2-1 and he's a very keen Man Utd supporter). This did bring a wry smile at break.

Then he entered fully into my April Fools' Day favourite. He had a tutorial period with Year 7, his own form. I entered the classroom carrying a large, official looking brown envelope. I announced that the Department for Education and Science required a simple spelling test for all 11-year-olds. The 'test' was very difficult. Nearly all scored 0 or 1 out of 10. I expressed my profound disappointment and then, when about to leave, I pretended to notice that the initial letters of the ten words in the test spelt 'April Fools' backwards. It went down very well for they were so gullible, with two exceptions. One spotted the ruse in the first minute but was silenced; while another very bright spark scored 6 out of 10 – he even had 'archaeology' correct.

Year 11, with only three weeks today to their leaving, are trying to slip their leads. It's a difficult balancing act between restraint and freedom. House assembly and my old house Jessop look likely to finish last yet again.

There was a foreshortened management meeting to discuss the Ofsted inspection – date now fixed for 4th November. A staff meeting followed in which Clive attempted to defuse the printing/duplicating controversy and then [split us] into groups to discuss 'environment'.

As the Senior Management Team stayed out of the discussion, I slipped home after 10 minutes. How naughty.

Tuesday 2nd April 1996

THE penultimate day of the spring term for pupils and restlessness definitely detectable. Staff, too, are ready. I noticed today how at the end of school they sat jadedly yawning in the staffroom. Outsiders will say "Two weeks' holiday, again! You lucky..." Insiders reply "Come and join us then."

I say, yet again, that if there were no such breaks there would not be a teaching profession. Pressures today are so great. And yet there are Rewards – I had two early on. A letter of apology from a Year 9 Classical Studies pupil who is a very irregular hander-in of homework. It was genuine and was very moving, clearly written from the heart. I shall add it to my store of farewell letters and notes. Modesty prevents my quoting it in detail but, simply put, it said "I shall miss you, you're a very good teacher".

Then on to Year 9 Latin which wasn't. Half [the class] were in France [on a school trip] so I gave my annual lesson on 'Time – Modern and Roman'. It was a pleasure to have a break from the language routine and they seemed to enjoy it thoroughly.

Year 11 Latin next. Some [pupils] superb, others disastrous. A couple are going to pieces it seems and I begin to doubt whether they will recover in time.

A lunchtime duet, Year 10 assembly and a cover lesson. Had a chat with S—— on the possibility of her applying for the pastoral post. But she's not interested.

Home to meet the estate agent.

Wednesday 3rd April 1996

SO the penultimate term is over, at least in terms of teaching. Yet tomorrow is a training day and tonight it is the Old Almondburians' Society executive meeting so I cannot feel I can begin to unwind, recharge and relax just yet. Even after tomorrow, I shall find it difficult with the house now at last officially on the market and presumably people showing some interest. If they don't, then that will be another worry. I envy three colleagues who will be in Spain and others elsewhere. Our turn will come before long.

For a final day, it was quite relaxed although I have at least eight names in my diary to 'see' on the first Monday back. However, I'll try to forget about them for two weeks.

I really enjoyed my Latin lesson this morning as I had to mark time, the group's parallel class having their lesson on a Thursday. I was on to my favourite topic of 'derivatives'. They lapped it up. What a marvellous feeling still to hold a group of young faces (metaphorically!) in one's hand. While doing the '-ines' – canine, bovine, taurine and the like – one boy even gave me 'vulpine' and with its correct meaning. Year 9 Classical Studies was also enjoyed, or so it appeared by teacher and taught. So happy that my teaching for the term finished on such a high note.

Then we were on to more serious matters as we discussed how to fill the pastoral posts. A little manoeuvering, and Machiavellian tactics are being used, but it's all for the 'Greater Good of the School' as we seek to salve our consciences.

The ITT students look very tired, the buses arrived on time, except the K.78, and I hurried home to meet my sister- in- law Jennie.

SUMMER TERM

Monday 22nd April 1996

THE Last Lap. The Final Stage. Whatever metaphor is chosen, the fact is that today is the start of my 105th and final term at King James's School and the last term of my full-time teaching career. A hint there that I may one day give another lesson, somewhere?

After a two-week break in which I enjoyed the undiluted pleasure of grandson's company for one week, when the weather was poor with snow again last Monday, worries over the paucity of would-be house purchasers and generally not feeling particularly well, this morning provided a sunny, warm walk to school.

I felt 'nervioso', as the Spanish would say – a mixture of apprehension and tension, and I felt an eagerness to banish immediate thoughts of dinners, speeches and farewells. The last lap of any race is always demanding and yet with a sprint finish it can pass quickly. So I resolved to throw myself into school matters wholeheartedly, to make no special plans and then it will soon be 19th July 1996.

Symbolically, I spent the first hour going through my room filling the waste paper basket and sifting through piles of papers and books. There will be a very big *lustrum* once Year 11 have gone. (In Roman times, this was a sacrificial purification – really a gigantic spring-clean every five years although in my case it will be 35). Plenty of news to catch up on from colleagues who have been away. The hustle and bustle of the staff room will be one thing I shall miss very much but not the pressures of the classroom and the corridor. I am trying to divert to the proper channels some matters which routinely come my way.

Two and a half hours of management meeting. Very intense and I found this very demanding, a contrast to yesterday's day of sunshine when I was at last able to sit out on our patio.

Tuesday 23rd April 1996

ONLY two days gone and already feeling some tension this evening although not particularly severe. Why? Just a busy day, I suppose, but with undertones of concern about the future of Latin at KJS, about retirement, house selling and purchase *et alia*. Yet how rapidly the days pass was vividly and movingly brought home by noting that today is the first anniversary of the death of former Head of English Mike Thornton. One year has passed and yet it seems so recent, his memory is so fresh. One year on and I'll have been retired for some eight months and I shall be a memory and unknown to Year 7s. *Sic transit gloria magistrorum*[1].

Clive mentioned in Briefing the occasion of my leaving and the consequent dinner on 12th July. Another poignant moment. Year 9 Latin was the last opportunity to push the subject for next year. I gave out a passage from the *Sunday Times* on the resurgence and value of Latin. I am aware that this could be construed as unprofessional but Latin has been taught on this site since 1608 and I should be upset if it were to cease soon after my departure. I reminded the pupils that subject preferences would have to be expressed in the next few days so it would be clearer by 4th May if a viable Latin set would exist for next year[2].

Year 11 followed. What a delightful group they are! I shall miss them and I do hope the feelings will be reciprocal. On Friday I must remember to take in my camera. Marked the exam practice test on Cicero and for the most part the results were excellent.

Year 11 are generally becoming restless with only 2½ weeks to go. It's a case of trying to keep the lid on a bubbling pot.

Met with C—— and L—— regarding the 1996-97 timetable. We were interrupted by our Bursar who informed me that W—— was having real problems, shouting very loudly and a pupil refusing to leave his lesson.

This has been happening for some 22 years, so what's new?

[1]*So passes the glory of schoolteachers*

[2]*Rather than choose their desired options for Year 10 (and hence GCSEs) from subject boxes, pupils were asked to list their preferences and then the boxes were formed to fit their wishes as far as possible. It was impossible to fulfil every request but with skilled timetablers it worked well. They now had the assistance of computer programmes – a far cry from the earlier days of paper, pencil and rubbers.*

056
DAYS TO GO

Wednesday 24th April 1996

ANOTHER significant day in the finality of things, but more of that later. By 8.45 am, the new senior management team was meeting; I (supernumerary) was also present. They were there to begin the re-allocation of jobs and to discuss how best to handle this tricky task.

Most of this I am happy about but when I went off to teach Year 8 Latin – a priority, as I see them only once a week for 35 minutes and

I do enjoy their company – discussion apparently turned to the construction of the timetable and criticism thereof. This was mainly levelled at C—— and L—— and it was reported unofficially to me by P——. I am very angry about this, for I am convinced they do an excellent job without sufficient recompense either financially or in time allowance. If they were to discover this criticism, I wouldn't be surprised if they justifiably suggested that the Senior Management Team should find someone else to do the job. There is some poor man management here and lack of sensitivity.

Year 9 Classical Studies was replaced by House cross-country. I enjoyed being out in the sunshine and then helping to record the results. It took me back to my much younger days when I was often involved in PE activities. What a microcosm of school life was displayed in their running or in some cases the walking; the skivers, the strugglers, the real triers, the determinedly successful and the really talented.

At lunch I had to ask Clive if I could take today's assembly. With exams coming up for Years 9 and 10 and GCSEs for 11, the sports hall will have desks in from Monday onwards. Therefore today was the last occasion when the whole school would be together. Self-indulgence? Would it go smoothly, having asked to take it? It would have been a sad memory if it had flopped.

Of course, it did not. I read my favourite Bible piece regarding the *Parable of the Talents* and for the last time explained that every single one of them had a talent of some kind which they should not hide but were morally obliged to develop. I finished with another of my favourite prayers which I call 'The Irish One'[1] and begins 'May the wind be always at your back.' [I said:] "God bless you all," and left to spontaneous applause, all very moving. I felt mightily relieved.

After school, I went down to the Huddersfield Town football ground at Leeds Road – how many hours I have spent there over the years ?– to see my last school soccer match. KJS were playing in a cup final; unfortunately they lost.

[1] *Traditional Irish blessing, authorship unknown*

Thursday 25th April 1996

IT'S 5.30 pm and I feel weary. I know this is becoming repetitive but there's no point in lying to my diary. There is a parents' meeting tonight, the very last one. It's Year 9, in which I teach three classes so it will inevitably be very busy. I'm double-booked from 6.30 pm onwards. This means three hours of rapid conversation. I know that (a) the time will fly and (b) I will be exhausted at the end. However, I have to remember that what I say can be of great significance to parents. It will no doubt be stored up, repeated and used in various ways. I wonder who will be the last ever parents? Shall I tell them?

Thank goodness tomorrow is Friday. Only one short lesson today, a Year 8 Latin; [meanwhile] Year 11s are definitely creating tension.

The Bretton College tutor is in to see one of our ITT student teachers who is failing. He's a delightful young man but it's a delicate, tricky situation. There have been numerous little disciplinary matters to sort out, including the old one of where a pupil buys a bus ticket, and then drops it out of the window to his friend below[1]. It happened again last night when I was on bus duty and two buses were held up for a considerable time. Smokers and transistor radio owners sent to me but I'm moving them on to their Heads of Year in my attempts to wean colleagues from their over-dependence on me before next September.

A smile at lunchtime when one pupil, sent by me to the Bridge (the area that links the Dorms and the new buildings and is used as a detention area) for kicking a litter bin. When I returned, there was a second pupil present. "I'm here 'cos you didn't see me, but I am guilty too."

So there is still a conscience around.

[1]*An occasional scam whereby a single purchased bus ticket could be used by more than one pupil, to the financial detriment of the bus company*

Friday 26th April 1996

THE present state of things, both mental and physical, is so different from that of two hours ago that in order to record the day's events through my teacher's eyes I shall have to do a little time-travelling. A glass of sherry followed by roast beef and accompanied by an excellent Rioja Reserva with a small *anis dulce* as a digestif have combined to put a different complexion on things completely and a distinctly rosy one to boot.

News that mother is definitely settled in a home added to the warm glow on Friday evening. There are now her house contents to dispose of but that's a comparatively minor problem.

So back to the school day. At 5.30 pm, yet again, I felt drained, more so than is usual on a Friday. Last night was as expected. In two hours and 50 minutes 38 sets of parents were seen. Generally it went well and [with] very kind words, and best wishes for retirement were often expressed. It seems that there is a good size Latin group forming for next year which will be under N——'s excellent tuition.

Who were to be my very last parents? As it turned out, it was the parents of an able boy but they were a somewhat arrogant pair. A pity but then I had no choice.

Today back at school within 10½ hours of leaving last night. Once under way, Year 9 Classical Studies went very well and Latin Year 11 ...as always. The last 10 minutes were taken up with photos of 'DAB's Last Latin Group'.

Marking furiously until lunch, hoping to have no books to take home for the weekend. A sing for 20 minutes at lunchtime with three Year 9 girls listening. Even with such an 'audience' the adrenaline flowed and we sang well. Ended the week with an extra bus duty in the sunshine and then supervising three Year 11s in an after-school detention until 4.00 pm. At least it meant I finished my marking.

There are only two weeks of Year 11 to go. We seem to be keeping the lid firmly on the bubbling pot ...so far.

Monday 29th April 1996

A REAL Monday morning feeling today brought on by a combination of concerns. Selling our house, sorting out mother's house, car rally to plan, Year 11 imminent leavers and feeling far from 100% physically. Yet, above all, I suspect it's the last lap syndrome, the final mile; I can see the tape or the winning post but resources are running low. Energy, and perhaps above all enthusiasm, are slipping away.

Yet I still want to finish on a high note, believing a proper job is being done. This afternoon, when asked by Clive to interview all curriculum team managers and check their curriculum documents[1] for next November's Ofsted inspection, I felt almost like shouting out, "No thanks. Move it on. Give it to next year's curriculum manager." But, of course, I did not and I must not. It's my job and I'm paid until the end of August. So, teeth gritted, I went off to see R——, whose wife is an Ofsted inspector, for guidance and assistance. Much valued help was generously offered and accepted.

Telephone conversations with some Year 11 parents, desperate that their offspring should conform or work harder even at this late stage. Interview all set up tonight with one student who needs every bit of help for an excellent apprenticeship which he has secured ...but he failed to appear. Others are making threatening noises about what they're going to do next week. It's probably just talk but it does sow ill ease.

I tried to cheer myself this morning by beginning ruthlessly to clear my room. What memories! An Oxbridge Latin entry paper; set books with detailed annotations; stacks of past papers – all seized and into the dustbin in a series of rapid sweeps. How many hours of work there!

Still, it's the end of one phase of life, clearing away for the next. So I tell myself.

[1]*Each subject department was required to produce a document setting out its teaching policy under various headings*

Tuesday 30th April 1996

BETTER ...but not better. Better, inevitably, because once into the week one is swept along by events, phone calls knocks on door, calls to lessons.

I realise that I didn't mention that yesterday began with a double cover for R——. Ill yet again. How many odd days off? Cynically, it could be said that facing Monday morning was too great a challenge. The group's books were not where they were supposed to be and the instructions were not particularly clear unless one actually taught the subject. So covering the lesson was quite a challenge. If you are going to be off, have the courtesy to make it easy for the one covering!

Today was much more satisfying in that I gave a good lesson to the rump of Year 9 Latin, (the rest were out on a Geography field trip). So I seized the opportunity to talk about two of my favourite subjects 'Roman deities' and the names of the planets in our solar system.

Then on to Year 11 Latin where there was plenty of good humour. Year 11 generally remain a problem and the two who failed to appear last night remain recalcitrant. One who needs extra tuition for his apprenticeship is reluctant to accept it and the other always feels victimised and yet desperately seeks attention.

Added to this, colleagues are more and more disturbed by threats of what will happen on the final day. What a contrast to the grammar school days when after exams pupils returned to do voluntary work in the local community. Clive now seems more willing to filter some off gradually[1], *pour encourager les autres.*

Highlight today was perhaps a 20 minute sing at lunchtime when all four were there and our leader T—— was ecstatic over our performance.

At the last minute, I discovered I was taking a Year 9 assembly but I enjoyed it in that I became anecdotal about 'true character emerging through adversity'. [It was] inspired by reports of yesterday's Geography field trip in pouring rain. How one used to get to know pupils better in one week at a wet scout camp than over seven years in the classroom! An exaggeration? I am sure that this is largely true.

Tomorrow is May Day and perhaps we should all be uplifted by warmer days.

[1]*Hint that their attendance at school was not perhaps 'absolutely' mandatory*

CHAPTER 9

May
1996

~ The death of my Mother ~

Wednesday 1st May 1996

HARDLY a 'May Day' from a meteorological standpoint. Cold, very heavy rain at times and those poor Year 9s on a field trip to Settle had their sheets, attached to clipboards, soon turned into a soggy mess. A premature return to school was enforced.

Despite the gloom, spirits are again a little higher today. Another solid night's unaided sleep, but I felt I could have used another hour; and then off to face Day 141. In some ways the 51 [days] to go sounds a lot and in other ways it sounds very little.

I began the day deliberately slowly, trying to take one thing at a time. There is little doubt that it is concurrent pressure from so many different quarters that causes stress. One demanding task to complete and then on to the next would make life so much easier – but school life just isn't like that any more. In 1961 it most certainly was so much less complicated. I was asked yesterday about the old staff room and smiled as I recounted how 21 people (all men, of course, and I was number 21) all crowded into a small room at break. Most smoked and quite a few pipes helped to increase the blue haze. Surnames were used by the older ones to address each other, tatty gowns were worn by nearly all and Bridge at lunchtime was played by the select few. Cigarettes left on the edges of the Bridge table left their black marks. If someone were to produce a cigarette in the staffroom today there would be an outcry.

Today in Year 8 Latin all went well except that the same pupil copied yet again. How bold or desperate!

In Year 9 Classical Studies we are running out of time, for the exams are due next week. I therefore summarised the main points for them on the blackboard. What an easy lesson that makes. All quietly scribbling away. It's not my style but I can see why some teachers still do a lot of it.

Bus duty in the rain, yet a record turnaround.

Languages panel meeting until 4.20 pm.

Thursday 2nd May 1996

IT'S 5.30 pm and it's suddenly all go. Badminton at 6.15; house viewers at 7.00 so the Hoover is out; local election so must vote; fire to light; diary to complete; and solve two clues in the *Daily Telegraph* crossword [the latter a] very low priority. All this after a comparatively lazy day.

'A lazy day?' Impossible. But therein lies much of the problem. As I don't feel under pressure I have time to look at the photographs of Northern Majorca taken by the Kirklees EWO (Education Welfare Officer, 'Truant Officer' in the old currency). It's an area we long to visit in the [bird] migration season. Then guilt floods in, and off I go looking for tasks (or looking for trouble, as Margaret would say).

I didn't record a conversation yesterday lunchtime with a top Year 9 girl who is not only struggling with her Preferences but also with her own admitted hypersensitivity. She is very intelligent, very pretty, very hard-working yet reacts strongly – that is passively – to any teasing or criticism by her peers. We had a very frank, very moving 15 minutes in which I felt I gave her some very sound advice about now and her future. She seemed very reassured, considerably cheered and at the end she thanked me; and I'm pretty sure she will always remember those 15 minutes. They could have a profound effect on her future. Such influences do we teachers have: frightening in many ways, so rewarding in others.

Quite a bit of time today spent clearing and arranging stuff in piles for handing on. But to whom? Still no moves in this area [and] with Ofsted due in November. Clive wants me to ensure documents are completed by Whitsuntide. This results in panic from some curriculum areas. Such piles of paper they have but is it of the right kind? I don't envy them and I'm very pleased to be escaping from this plethora of paper.

Temperature today 5° C but my spirits are rising.

Friday 3rd May 1996

ANOTHER week has passed by more rapidly than the last one and only 49 days to go as I write and so much still to do, to pass on. Still weighing heavily on me are the policy documents required for Ofsted which some colleagues have yet to write and all of which I have to check, the final date being the end of this half term. Another task to sap the energy .

Yet for a long time now I have had to view myself as an administrator rather than a teacher but those in management usually agree that the greatest pleasure is to be derived from being in the classroom. All this documentation has to be done to satisfy government regulations but I shall be happy to leave this aspect of teaching, or rather education, a long way behind.

Today started with difficulty; it had been a bad night, up at 4.00 am and then solidly asleep when the alarm went at 6.40 am. Going to school I noticed a Year 11 girl wearing tight jeans. Do I get involved? Fortunately, I said nothing as it turned out to be a 'non-uniform day' to raise money for Dunblane. I had forgotten but so had most of my other senior colleagues.

I felt really groggy during first lesson and struggled for the first half hour. Year 11 Latin all present for the final 'unseen' under exam conditions. After about 20 minutes S——, spokesperson and boldest of the pupils said, "Sir, are you sure this is the right vocabulary sheet?". It wasn't – again.[1] What a shambles on my part. Time to retire! Nevertheless, I have marked the first six and they are going to be the best work yet. A real morale-booster for them and for me.

An Old Almondburian, 1959 leaver, arrived at 11.45 am and although I planned to spend only 10 minutes with him I enjoyed his company and recollection of staff of that era so much it became 45.

The Year 11 [pupils]? Three have now taken the King James's equivalent of an early bath. And the atmosphere has certainly improved; comparative calm prevails. Also reassuring was the numbers who are opting for Latin next year. A solid 15 it seems including Little Miss Nose Stud.

You can never tell and must never pre-judge.

[1]*See 15th March 1996*

162

MONDAY 6TH MAY 1996:
BANK HOLIDAY

Tuesday 7th May 1996

AFTER yesterday's holiday today should've been like a Monday. But it wasn't. Because of the long weekend? Because the day is actually Tuesday and that Monday morning feeling is not transferable?

Straight into teaching Year 9 Latin, a good lesson as they were all present and I was buoyed up by the sound group [that is] forming for next year. Year 11 Latin [had] four missing, most unusual, but then I realised they are already involved in other GCSE exams. This was after 2½ hours marking their last 'unseen' over the weekend. Generally they had done very well. So we enjoyed a lovely atmosphere and plenty of good humour.

After break, things declined with our Year 9 problem boy who I feel needs help far greater than we, in a normal school situation, can give him. Rocking, kicking, screaming and sobbing until I eventually managed to calm him down but all very demanding. I contacted his father – there is a broken home – but I don't really know where we go from here.

Year 11, with three departed, are much calmer at lunchtime but Jack and I called from our dinner as [there were] intruders on the premises with twelve of our own Year 11s. The situation was calmly dealt with and all dispersed. Three days for them left.

The two girls whom I noticed were absent last Wednesday I suspected were truanting. Their tutor had done nothing despite reports that one had been seen in the village in uniform. A more senior teacher was called in to investigate and discovered that one, a 13-year-old, has been going to her 18-year-old boyfriend's flat during the day. The poor parents were distraught but declared her tutor 'useless'. Why is the tutor not being hauled over some very hot coals?

Preferences [are] almost all in but, as always some groups, are too large while others are hardly viable. B—— is so excellent in this area; he must continue to practise his expertise.

Hardly seen Clive today. Is there any significance in this?

Wednesday 8th May 1996

A BETTER night's sleep than on Monday when I had been awake at 3.00 am. Pre-school tension after such a short break? Last night was an OAS executive meeting, poorly attended. Tonight is the OAS Quiz[1] from 7.30 to 9.30 pm and tomorrow night OAS badminton. What a large amount of time 'the Society'[2] takes up in my life. Add to that, time spent on it during the day and it really does mount up. At the moment it's a particularly pleasant part of the work as I welcome imminent Year 11 leavers into the Society and wish them well. What will outstanding student R—— be doing in 20 years' time? I do so hope that through the newsletters I can keep in contact with some of my students.

This is why I suppose I felt distinctly ill at ease in this morning's management meeting. I do feel that Clive is shortsighted regarding the OAS. There is so much goodwill there and enormous potential financial support. Yet lack of empathy and some give-and-take, exacerbated by penny-pinching, is going to destroy the relationship between school and Society completely unless a more sympathetic path is trod.

Also, attempts to clamp down on Year 11 jinks on the last day – in my opinion innocent ones – could backfire and cause more trouble. Still, I am trying very hard to bite my lip and not upset anyone.

[I was] observed by an ITT student [teacher] in Year 9 Latin and later gave an excellent seminar on 'Ancillary Staff'. Well, I thought it was excellent and they seemed fascinated.

Year 9 SATs[3] and invigilation of same. Shall I ever forget how slowly time passes as one patrols the long lines of desks?

Phone rang at 6.30 pm. News that mother is very ill and most probably dying. Deep breath, again.

[1] *Long-established annual Quiz Evening organised by the Old Almondburians' Society*

[2] *The Old Almondburians' Society, set up in 1920 with the specific objective of supporting the school and upholding its status*

[3] *National Curriculum assessments carried out in schools in England, colloquially known as Standard Attainment Tests. Since 2008, these assessments have been limited to primary schools.*

Thursday 9th May 1996

A WEARYING day. Assisted sleep meant that I woke some-what refreshed. It was just after 10.00 pm when I returned from school last night. A poorly attended Quiz Evening but an hilarious, highly enjoyable occasion for all present.

Nevertheless, domestic matters hung heavily. I telephoned the home early to be told they expected mother to live for only a few more days. So sad that this coincides with such a busy, stressful time at school but I have tried to remain as busy as possible.

Marked for an hour, taught a lively lesson to Year 8 and discussed curriculum documents with L——. He really is most helpful.

Some corridor patrolling. Year 11 again comparatively calm and generally very pleasant. A few visits from those wishing me well and requesting an autograph. Two came to warn me that a stinkbomb – "We've seen it!"– is destined for my room tomorrow. They seem genuinely concerned. I shall have to be on my guard.

Clive attempted to forestall shirt-signing by allowing non-uniform for Year 11 tomorrow. Many have already been signed and they plan non-uniform tomorrow: jeans and to-be-signed or already-signed school shirt. I await his reaction with interest. What a far cry all this is from my early days when examinees took exams in full school uniform, returned to school after exams and didn't leave until the last day of term. The good old, bad old days.

Tonight back to school for badminton. My second home – or first, according to Margaret.

Friday 10th May 1996

MOTHER died and Year 11 left. I taught my last GCSE Latin lesson. Many tears shed and feelings, often disguised, outpoured. Having preserved a safe distance from pupils for so long, it was a great relief to be able to display one's more intimate thoughts. To be able to show genuine pupil-teacher or teacher-pupil affection, to share moments of warmth, sadness, compassion and gratitude with young people with whom hundreds of hours have been spent over five years has left me again emotionally drained.

I received the telephoned news that mother's death was imminent at lunchtime and told this to close colleagues. In turn, I asked them to pass it on to the senior pupils in the Latin class so that they would understand why I had not been as buoyant in their last lesson as I should have liked. Again, they came to my room in tearful embraces and I was more moved than I have ever been in thirty-five years of teaching, as though a great outburst of pent up love for pupils could at last be released. Inevitably these days, some pupils had brought in drink, were badly behaved and were sent away. The vast majority were excellent and little or no damage was done. Imagine having to be grateful for that!

Year 11 brought me wine, champagne, a book, a giant card and individual ones. Final assembly with them and more tears and signings and best wishes and home to a telephone call at 4.30 pm to say mother had died at 4.15.

Tomorrow 'home'.

Monday 13th May 1996

AND suddenly it's Monday morning and it's a glorious day, warm at last. Although this diary is intended to be a record of my last school year, external events do so intrude into the working day that they become inseparable. The weekend, however, superficially at least, soon was forgotten as it disappeared under a series of happenings, visits etc.

Clive was in my room by 8.15 am offering his condolences; by 8.20 am I was taking a phone call regarding Year 10 Preferences; and by 8.25 am I was marking Year 8 books. I stayed out of the staffroom deliberately. Pat was touchingly kind. Thank goodness for such people.

At 10.30 am there was a phone call to say an Old Almondburian was downstairs and wishing to visit. I played my usual trick by asking for his name. Quickly I looked up his index card in my room and then went down to greet him by his first name. "Your father was a doctor and you used to live in Milnsbridge." His name was Dr Elphinstone Forrest Gilmour, an eminent entomologist[1]. It turned out to be another very precious half hour. Charming man, full of stories and appreciation and, of course, even though he is 74 we both knew teachers such as Addy, Gledhill, Hudson and Haigh[2] as they overlapped his going and my arriving. He joined the OAS and bought a History[3].

A Year 9 pupil asked, "Is it true, sir, your mother has only 24 hours to live?" I explained that she had died last Friday and sorrow was expressed. Another pupil asked "Is it okay for Martin to buy you a card, sir?" "Sniff".

Very full management meeting from 2.30 to 4.30 pm but I am still fearful of a school/OAS split when I go. I do wish Clive would be a little more flexible and could see how much goodwill can so easily be lost. Or is it I who am being shortsighted and biased? I shall be pleased to escape all this intrigue.

[1]*Noted British entomologist (b. in Ayrshire, 8th September 1922) who attended King James's Grammar School from 1933 to 1939. Died 14th February 2008.*
[2]*Former KJGS teachers of French, Music, Geography and PE respectively*
[3]*A History of King James's Grammar School in Almondbury by Gerald Hinchliffe (The Advertiser Press Ltd/1963)*

Tuesday 14th May 1996

043

DAYS TO GO

MY adult Spanish class last night and then phone calls from a couple who are seriously interested in buying our house. It left me again feeling physically very tired but mentally so alert that I could not face bed until 11.30 pm.

Not surprisingly, this has meant I felt tired again today. So much so that I have tried to turn a blind eye on certain occasions although I do find this unfortunately very hard to do. Had sympathy cards left on my desk and one brought personally by a Year 9 pupil, the one who had previously written the "Sorry you're leaving letter" – a likeable little rascal.[1]

I must record the girl from last Friday who came to complain she had found a hair in her dinner. I questioned whether she had been expecting rabbit. I have been awaiting a phone call from her mother along the lines of, "How dare you be so flippant to my daughter?" But so far nothing has been forthcoming.

The real point is [that it's] a reflection on our complaining, compensation-seeking-I-know-my-rights society. She was offered a completely fresh meal – but refused. I can imagine what would have happened 25 years ago but then again I can't, because it simply would not have arisen.

Today was 'Forward Planning Day', reallocating tasks and responsibilities for next year. It started frustratingly slowly, as 20 minutes or more were spent fixing future possible meeting times. By 12.40 pm, four hours later, 1996–97 was beginning to take shape. It was all tiring for me as I felt dull but I do hope I made a few useful contributions.

More this afternoon on Ofsted documents. Year 9 Latin and Classical Studies this afternoon were a comparative relief. I shall positively enjoy the routine of marking this evening.

[1]*See 2nd April 1996*

Wednesday 15th May 1996

AWAKE at 5.00 am. The thought that we have fewer than three months to find a new home jolted me into a state of wide-awakeness. Last night a sale [was] agreed at the asking price, no chain and a gentleman's agreement. The purchaser is the Professor of Architecture at the University of Huddersfield. All this has happened so quickly that, when added to all the recent happenings, it means that I have to face school and its demands with mind spinning. It was difficult to focus clearly.

Despite that, I gave a really good lesson to Year 8 Latin and I know they enjoyed it . How boastful that sounds and yet to me it is so important. It was the only lesson of the day as Year 9 are on internal exams. H—— remarked at the end of the day how for the past four weeks he has been so drowned in paperwork and oral examinations that his teaching is suffering. He is not giving good lessons and he is an outstanding teacher. He admits he is less tolerant with his pupils. What a shame and what a condemnation of the system. "Let the teachers teach!" has always been my cry and would remain so if I were taking up a crusade. B——, Maths teacher, calculates it costs more to examine one pupil in Maths Sats than he receives per annum for that pupil in capitation. Can this be justified?

Today mostly spent marking Year 9 Latin and Classical Studies exam papers which I started last night. Some 80 scripts of very varied abilities. The potential Latin candidates for Year 10 have done very well and I'm very pleased.

The tutor from Bretton College was in and we have to decide whether to fail or pass one struggling student [teacher]. In the end it was the school's decision. We – or I – took the easy way out and passed her. I could write a page on our dilemma. Such a crucial life-affecting and future pupil-affecting decision.

From 3.15 pm I talked to subject heads about Ofsted policy documents. How pleased and relieved I was when that was over.

Thursday 16th May 1996

A BETTER night but an unusual day in that it was not spent at school, rather on a Year 10 Geography field trip. I had not really given it much thought since being invited by B——, ten days ago, to join him. I had readily accepted, having enjoyed a similar one a number of years ago,

To school at the usual time but by 8.35 am we were leaving the car park with 21 students of very mixed ability. Although B—— was doing this trip for the third time this week and for the nth time over the years I was very impressed by his excellent organisation. The questionnaires were very well produced and his manner and lively approach were exemplary. Despite all his domestic difficulties he is to be admired for relegating all those in the face of the demands of teaching: a real professional in that sense.

Various stops to study land development, industrial sites, heather moors and so slowly on to Castleton. How different the atmosphere when pupils are in 'civvies' and out of the classroom. Far more relaxed and natural. It was unfortunate that the weather was bitingly cold especially up Winnats Pass[1]. The wind chill must have reduced the temperature to near freezing so certain stops had to be abandoned or curtailed.

On our return to Castleton the pupils surveyed the village, while the staff enjoyed coffee and soup in a pleasant café. Did we feel a little bit guilty?

I suddenly realised that this would be my very last school trip. I thanked the pupils for their cheerful company on this special visit. They responded movingly.

[1]*Mountain pass located between the small towns of Hope and Sparrowpit in the High Peak area of the Peak District*

Friday 17th May 1996

STILL feeling very weary this morning but for the most part it is self-inflicted, the result of two most strenuous games of badminton against Peter Griffin last night. They lasted an amazing length of time and for the first time ever he won both games and I felt absolutely whacked.

Slept soundly but Year 9 Classical Studies did not have the benefit of a lively, enthusiastic teacher to return their exam papers at 8.40 am. Indeed, I did wonder if it really mattered. For, despite being a lovely and lively group, the answers had so often been pathetic in the literal sense of the word. Question: 'Do you believe the Trojan War actually happened? Give evidence for your answer.' 'The Trojan War did happen because it was on the news that very night' (and I have corrected the spelling).

This rivals, in the first year of the comprehensive school, the following: 'Describe the flight of Aeneas from the burning Troy'. This led to a homework in which the pupil described Aeneas packing his case and catching a plane to fly, I think it was, to London.

This leaves me asking myself what they have gained – a rather basic question at the end of one's career. Yet I feel I am being unfairly simplistic in that two of the 13 did very well and showed ability and flair way above [the bottom] Set 6 of 6. There were two papers which were the equal of the first 10 I've marked in Set 3 which raises the [accuracy] of setting techniques or even the desirability of setting[1].

A busy day generally but I found time for a short sing at lunchtime. Unfortunately felt too tired to perform well. We need a lot of practice before our European Evening[2] later in the term.

Saw N—— regarding Ofsted documents. [We] two old stagers agree.

"However did we manage in the olden days? So much energy now goes into producing piles of paper."

Saw the most able girl in Latin Year 9. I think I have convinced her of her brilliance and I think she'll change her option from Drama to Latin. Am I being unprofessional? She is so modest and I wonder where she will be in twenty years' time?

[1] *With an intake of around 180 pupils a year it was necessary to arrange them in 'Sets' according to academic ability, so Set 6 of 6 was ostensibly the weakest group*

[2] *An evening's entertainment in which pupils and staff could show off their language, singing and dancing skills*

Monday 20th May 1996
Mother's funeral

Tuesday 21st May 1996
IN a year's time I hope I can look back from some sun-kissed beach or simply from a sunny spot in the Southwest and think how relaxed and fit I feel. Yet one year ago today I was feeling so strained that going round Sainsbury's all I wanted to do was to get home.

Not that this condition is brought on by school alone. Yesterday was a very dignified, very moving, perfect send-off for mother and it's not the purpose of this diary to record the details. Yet inevitably that and just 'looking in' on my last Spanish evening class exacerbated the feeling. I have been taking this evening class at Huddersfield Technical College for 17 years, a real escape at times and very rewarding. I received many kind words and presents but it meant that this morning I began feeling weary and finished feeling shattered. That yawning exhaustion I have known so well.

A pity, for it was a beautiful, still morning and there were Year 9 Latin [pupils] waiting for their exam results which were generally very good. I so wanted them to sense I was very pleased with them and sad not to be taking them on to GCSE. Six [of them] were missing, visiting the University of Huddersfield. No doubt worthwhile but still very annoying to be missing such a lesson after so much time had been spent marking. "Too much time away from the classroom [for] both pupils and staff" would be one of my major complaints of the last decade.

One hour supervising a higher Spanish GCSE paper which I thought (and Head of Languages confirmed), was 'demanding'. Catching up for the next hour, an early lunch and then management [discussion on] 'The Future' from 1.00 until 4.00 pm with two short breaks. Yawn! I know I should have been more involved but so much talk, paper and tiredness meant the clock ticked by very slowly.

Let's hope I feel brighter tomorrow.

Wednesday 22nd May 1996

SO much better! Still tired tonight but that completely washed-out feeling has at last gone. Another good night's sleep has helped but also 'Curriculum Panel'[1] is over and that is a relief.

This morning was dominated by arrangements for the Head of English post. I had the simple task of showing the four candidates around the school in separate pairs, a job I enjoy and feel I do it well, having known the place for so long. Unfortunately, it meant that I had to miss Year 8 Latin, my weekly 30 minute slot, and I shan't see them again until after half term. It's surprising how the candidate can talk himself or herself out of or into a job on such a deceptive little tour. Unguarded comments are stored up and one candidate talked almost incessantly to the point where neither I nor his fellow candidates could get a word in. He would have been intolerable in meetings and I believe I confirmed what others felt later. The quieter, more relaxed approach is definitely to be recommended.

I did teach Year 9 Classical Studies, or rather returned their exam papers which for a Set 3 were generally disappointing. Any idea of solid revision and assimilation of facts seems foreign to the majority. A direct onslaught could have been used but I didn't want to leave too sour a taste.

Took a Year 8 assembly and there, too, I was concerned. They do seem an ill-disciplined year, possibly the result of the National Curriculum and so much emphasis on group work. K—— and I agreed that by Year 11 they are going to be very difficult but by then we will both be far away and shall be able to make "I told you so" noises.

After bus duty, I rushed back to a Curriculum Panel meeting which I was to chair. I confess I've never felt at ease with these sessions and although outwardly I may appear calm and in control, inwardly I'm also very apprehensive. Still, a workmanlike and cheerful atmosphere prevailed ...and it was my last!

[1] *The Curriculum Panel, chaired by DAB, met approximately every month. Comprising the head of each subject area – maths, science, technology, languages, humanities etc – it took the form of a wide-ranging discussion on matters directly related to the teaching of these subjects.*

Thursday 23rd May 1996

036 DAYS TO GO

AT 11.35 am I handed over to Jack [Taylor] the Presentation Evening file, or rather files. This was an historic moment in that, at last, I have begun to pass on tasks to others for '96–'97. As this will be Jack's last year it is only a stopgap measure but it's a start. Many more yet to complete.

Last night C—— and I had been to the YMCA sports complex at Birchencliffe. This was to arrange a venue for the staff car rally supper. There I met two Old Almondburians, both wealthy and with much worldly experience; one of whom, his friend quietly revealed, is a multimillionaire. I remember him vaguely as a rather ordinary pupil in the early '60s and here I am retiring after 35 years on a salary around £30,000. This morning I tried to contact him and to invite him to help the school in some capacity. Still feeling weary but I'm coming to accept I've got to live with this until retirement. Or it could be simply old age?

Too snappy with Year 8 [pupils] so had to use humour to relieve a tense atmosphere. At 11.45 am Ken Leech[1] and his wife, Janine from Melbourne, Australia arrived. I have been receiving them for some years now so this was to be the last visit while I'm still around in Huddersfield. It is always a most pleasant occasion and we have a very strong invitation to visit Oz[2]. He related how 12 from his year of 60 pupils (he is now 60) had been summoned to *The Croppers Arms*[3] by phone call for a social evening – all through the OAS. I'm very proud of my part in all this. There was a Senior Management Team meeting for 1¼ hours after school in which we discussed new roles and I played my Nestorian part[4].

An internet connection with our sister school in France is being established and I thought what a far cry it was from headmaster of KJGS, Harry Taylor, and his 'short-circuit television'.

[1] *Former King James's Grammar School pupil 1947-52*
[2] *DAB visited Australia with grand-daughter Anna in 2012*
[3] *Popular traditional Yorkshire pub in Marsh, Huddersfield*
[4] *Nestor was the legendary wise king of Pylos described in Homer's* Odyssey

Friday 24th May 1996

035
DAYS TO GO

THE last day of the penultimate half term and in mathematical terms 104/105ths of my time at KJS are behind me. A week now to go house hunting in the Southwest as a call to the solicitor this morning suggested that all is progressing well and an agreed sale could be signed in two weeks' time. This gave a boost to the morning. I had been doing the *Daily Telegraph* crossword at 5am!

Year 9 bottom set Classical Studies did not suffer as we had, I felt, an interesting lesson on Ancient Greek Social Life and particularly their dress compared with modern times. Some pupils remain very naive. "Did the ancient Greeks have rubber sandals cut out from old car tyres?" The rest of the class, of course, didn't laugh or mock even if they realised the absurdity of the question. That's a very pleasant aspect of the least able pupils.

My attempts to get the multimillionaire up to school need more support as, I suspect, he smells a financial rat – not surprising really. Went round to see the ITT students and even the weaker ones are improving. This is vital as their time with us is nearly up.

The lunch hour saw at last half an hour's sing but R—— failed to appear again so it was only a trio. Did some more clearing of my shelves. Well annotated 'A' level texts with pages of notes interleaving were sorted through. How many hours of work and study they represented but in most instances it was a case of 'Into the bin' for they are of little use and certainly highly unlikely to be used again. They would only gather more dust. Sad but inevitable.

At the end of the afternoon I did a demonstration 'End of Lesson Routine' for two comparatively inexperienced science teachers. Will they learn from it? Saw W—— regarding next year's timetable when he will be expected to have a support class for less able pupils[1]. This was not well received: "Unexpected, impossible, sorry." Yet it has to be.

I am trying not to upset colleagues or too many pupils in these final days but it's not easy at times. A week's break coming up which will not really be a holiday but may help to recharge the batteries.

[1]*Additional classes for less able pupils provided by teachers with spare periods in their timetables*

HALF-TERM BREAK

CHAPTER 10

June
1996

– Cricket in full swing – to Jack's delight –

Monday 3rd June 1996

BREAKING down my career into units of half terms, this morning I began the 210th and final part. Will the last lap be the hardest? Half term was spent house-hunting in the south-west but produced more confusion than clarification. On our return, seeing a 'Sold Subject to Contract' sign outside our house, I felt that concentration on school matters might prove difficult.

[But], as always, once caught up in the hurly-burly of everyday life at school such matters are immediately thrust into the background. I've noticed before how general elections, major disasters, deaths, crises etc are all soon ignored in the staffroom and are replaced by discussion of classroom trivia. Small-minded teachers or dedicated professionals?

Still chilly, but the promise of a mini-heatwave soon added a spring to my step. By 8.15 am I was shuffling papers on my desk and refreshing my memory of tasks left undone before half term. Called in the exam room – all Year 11 were in – to remind them of joining the OAS and to invite Year 11 Latin to see photos taken in our last lesson and to pick up revision sheets. They duly arrived in twos and threes after their exam and I did enjoy their comments and company in an informal atmosphere; this I shall miss.

I was infuriated by the news that over half term two of our five oak benches in the grounds, so carefully preserved and maintained over 10 years, have been taken and sawn up along with a number of small trees. The culprits then put them on a fire during the night; presumably they were cold and therefore we must sympathise.

Management meeting this afternoon. Much revolved around the introduction of internet links with Cork and St Dizier – and more and more technology. How old fashioned I am! It reminds me of the advent of language laboratories which were to revolutionise the teaching of Modern Languages. Their demise was quite rapid. I believe that teacher-pupil interaction is far more important but then I'm out of touch.

Tuesday 4th June 1996

AN amazing conversation this afternoon between Margaret and two KJS pupils (Years 7 and 9) which was carried on through the tamarisk hedge in our front garden in Foxglove Road. This encapsulated much of what is being felt and sometimes said at the moment.

It lasted some five minutes and began, "Are you Mrs Bush?" It followed the lines of "When Mr Bush goes it'll be a shambles." I'm flattered but concerned. They were essentially polite but it also illustrates the point that I've made before, that today's pupils may lack respect and awe but in other ways are gratifyingly more natural.

It has been a very hectic day, something like eight phone calls this afternoon in 90 minutes although some were personal rather than school related. However, it is not easy to separate school and home life at the moment.

The day started at 4.30 am. After last night's OAS meeting which again gave rise to a possible school/OAS schism[1], I woke in a cold sweat for I dread such a happening after so many years of building up such a close relationship. It concerns me that the school is not prepared to give more and I lay the blame firmly at the door – or doors – of two people.

Year 9 Latin were as delightfully lively as ever. I was very lucky to be asked by S—— to switch from exam room supervision to act as an amanuensis for a pupil with a broken or dislocated shoulder. I had completely missed my name on the supervision list. Slipping!

Policy documents for Ofsted are starting to come in. If I stayed longer I am sure I should perish under a surfeit of same.

Half an hour's sing at lunchtime was a relief and then hurriedly back to work out Preferences for Year 10 with B——.

I have just remembered how the day began, with an attempted but failed arbitration between two Year 11 girls. One, a known thief, had been seen going into the other's bag and £6 was missing. It was vehemently denied and she left, shouting and bawling, to take her GCSE Maths exam. I don't think it would make much difference to her result.

Talked to Clive for 45 minutes regarding the OAS and his proposed trip to France with P—— to set up links. I told him that I thought it was ill-advised[2].

[1]*A long-running investigation led by the Old Almondburians' Society into suspected mismanagement of the school's ancient bequests by Kirklees Borough Council; resolved in 2004 when the Council agreed to pay a very large sum in settlement.*

[2]*Ill-advised in terms of the cost of a four-day trip in relation to the likely benefits.*

Wednesday 5th June 1996

THE car alarm going off, unprovoked, during the night when I was at my deepest, meant an interruption during a much needed sleep. Consequently, a day of yawns especially during our Senior Management Team meetings. I was in the first one by 8.45 am but found the pace infuriatingly slow. It's all right being democratic but leaders are paid to lead, and snappier delegation and decision-making would have been my style. Even with another one hour and 10 minutes after break we are still only halfway through next year's calendar and still none of my responsibilities has been reallocated. What an annoyance!

Nipping off to teach Year 8 Latin and then Year 9 Classical Studies was a blessed relief. This proves either that teaching is still the most important job or that I was never intended to be a Head.

The Classical Studies lesson, which I was not really looking forward to in my weary state, turned out to be a *tour de force*. It was largely unplanned but turned into a really good discussion on ancient Greek houses, dress, furniture etc and comparison with modern times.

At lunch, I was so disappointed when the top Year 9 Latin student declared she had finally decided to do Art instead of Latin. In 1961 there would have been no choice. The 'A' stream did Latin and 'B' stream Art. And of course that was wrong and today's system is so much better – but personal opinions have to be thrust aside.

Spent 20 minutes only with the ITT student [teachers] but as ever they were enjoyable. I had to clear mounds of paper before beginning and pointed out to them, perhaps again, that over the last 35 years I've seen a crippling amount of the stuff wearing me down.

Out to buses and I realised the other five colleagues were letting me do all the work. So I slipped away to see how they coped. Of course, they did. Then slipped away again, for tonight it's the second stage of planning the staff car rally.

I remember how earlier today a pupil sent to me for bad behaviour said that his father was no longer at home and his mother was on holiday in Greece.

Thursday 6th June 1996

THE most hectic day for quite some time produced that feeling of going under with so many things happening almost simultaneously. The warmest day of the year, coincidently. Surely this did not cause some short tempers and frayed nerves.

An early phone call from an irate neighbour regarding breaking down of a wall, litter and the stoning of a horse. Clive passed it on to me and the husband answered. Fortunately, I know him from my morning walk down Grasscroft and it turned into a pleasant chat. He even plays an occasional game of cricket with Jack. Who will pick up such issues next year without my local knowledge?

C—— then arrived at my room in a furious temper He has been allocated a new room while his own is being decorated. Unfortunately, his ex-wife had been put into the same room. She was banished to the lab and he moved in.

A report arrived that two of our Year 8 girls were sunbathing in a field off Sharp Lane. They were eventually tracked down. One is already 'beyond parental control'. How does the school then deal with her? And three more years of schooling to come?

My own Year 8 Latin [class] had been moved to a lab. The door was locked. Key borrowed and key stuck in lock. Frustration and embarrassment ensued.

Which reminds me. The Art Department policy document stated 'Pupils' spelling is corrected in such a way as not to cause them embarrasment (sic)'.

Trying to mark, shuffle option groups, see ITT student teachers regarding their external examiners, phone the *Huddersfield Examiner* regarding publicity for next Monday. Then a working lunch again. It lasted one hour which I feel I could have [been] consolidated into 20 minutes.

Clive is facing problems over the very unprofessional behaviour of two of our more militant colleagues who walked out of S——'s meeting when they considered time was up.

A problem with a Year 11 pupil who wrote obscenities on a French GCSE paper. I was not informed if they were in English or French.

Seeing colleagues tomorrow whose timetables will show changes for '96/'97 when schedules are re-distributed. This mainly is the result of cuts in our budget.

Tricky, but with touches of humour I feel I am getting there.

Friday 7th June 1996

ONE week of the final half term over already. As often, in some ways it seems to have slipped by so quickly; in others, especially when I feel so weary, it almost dragged. Year 9 bottom set Classical Studies was again a pleasure. They are so pleasantly simple – simple in no way pejorative. It's usually those with a little bit more ability who cause disciplinary problems.

The lesson was interrupted by the arrival of Old Almondburian, Steve Manning[1] and the two new updated honours boards. This has been a long-term project which I had cherished and here at last it has come to fruition.

After that, another very busy time. Policy documents [for Ofsted] are arriving in numbers and to read and correct these is a very time-consuming business. Pupil preferences have had to be put on one side but thanks to C—— and L—— timetable-scheduling is underway. It brought S—— to my room in high dudgeon again. So much teaching had not been expected. Obviously it means being tied to a classroom, less running around with a piece of paper, less sitting by the telephone. But there goes the cynic again. The same applies, I suppose, to other senior staff for 'Administration Posts' already means less and less direct contact with pupils through teaching.

The highlight, if one can call it such, of the lunch hour was a report of an Almondbury High School pupil on the site armed with an air pistol.

The police were sent for. I was not directly involved but Clive, already over-stretched today, had to abandon a Head's meeting this afternoon as this business took up most of his already short time.

Delighted to be able to tell S—— that she would have more teaching time next year. I believe the money is needed and I felt like God distributing *manna*. What a hubristic comparison. Year 7 assembly which I took for Clive, afforded an opportunity to ask about last Wednesday's through- the-hedge conversation. It turned out that one of the two was a Year 7 [pupil] generally regarded as a little pest. I was amazed.

This bears out the old adage (is 'old' tautological?): 'Never judge a book by its cover'.

[1]*King James's School 1976-81*

Monday 10th June 1996

BETWEEN 12.45 and 2.05 pm was one of those times when I wish I could have had a video camera covering my move-ments. I would then play it back periodically during my re-tirement so that I could appreciate fully the difference between the so hec-tic 'then' and the halcyon 'now'. Only 1 hour 20 minutes, admittedly, but I feel I crammed into that time about three hours normal work. It left me with that so familiar feeling. In a year's time, when spectacles are assuming an even deeper rosy hue, I shall need to remind myself that life then was at times almost unbearably busy and the relaxed life of retirement is definitely preferable. What was going on? It doesn't really matter. I just remember going over curriculum policy documents with W—— and B——, taking phone calls from the *Huddersfield Examiner*, seeing a number of pupils sent by the LTAs, discussing preference list with R——. It was a flood of matters supposedly needing 'immediate attention'.

The day had started quite calmly. Four references for ITT student [teachers] required by 10.00 am but mainly it is simply a question of up-dating. I saw A—— and C—— over their policy documents. Considering how much time they have obviously put in to the compilation of these, I felt almost guilty making any criticism. However, they accepted it very willingly and I wondered if they were expecting more.

By 11.20 am three Old Almondburians and a *Huddersfield Examiner* photographer had arrived to record the official handing over of the updated honours boards. [It shows] three 'ordinary' grammar school boys who have done so very well in the business world. Yet we must remember that, at that time, they were in the top 20 percentile academically. One [of them] has just bought a house for over half a million pounds and another's car appeared more expensive than our house. Still, as Margaret often says, "We didn't *have* to be teachers."

Management meeting from 2.00 to 3.10 pm and a staff meeting until 4.30 pm. Lots of exciting developments for '96/'97.

And for me, but elsewhere.

Tuesday 11th June 1996

I NOTICED yesterday that there are now fewer than 30 days to go. Now that does begin to sound very few. I am more and more convinced that I shall be ready, for there are so many trends that I find difficult to accept and I cannot decide if this is cynicism born of old age – comparatively – or realism born of experience. In simple terms, I can't accept, for example, that Clive and P—— flying to Paris next Tuesday, hiring a car and staying in a hotel for four days, all to set up internet links with our twin school in eastern France, will justify the expenditure. Yet at last night's staff meeting there were pleas to turn off the lights when leaving rooms and an announcement that capitation is going to be cut again. I know the French expedition is funded from external sources but the principle stands.

I mention again language labs and the revolution they were to bring to modern language teaching. I believe there are none now in existence. One day the teaching wheel will be reinvented and the teacher standing in front of a class, with all [pupils] listening and learning, will be the Great Pedagogical Revolution.

And what else has happened today? I confidently expect a phone call tomorrow from an irate mother who had instructed her son that it was not his job to wipe dining room tables as a punishment. He had decided that this gave him permission not to appear for me at 12.30 pm on the

Bridge. I interrupted him just as he was about to receive his dinner and marched him back to the same. All very upsetting and then he refused to have any dinner at all. Interfering parents! In the '60s he would have received a domestic clip round the ear for his abuse of the LTA in the first place.

At the end of the day I was upset by the news that a Year 9 girl, very sweet natured, has left KJS to be with her real mother after suffering abuse from her step-parent.

Wednesday 12th June 1996

A DAY of very mixed emotions, added to by concerns about mother who, it appears, has had a heart attack. Also concerns or problems about a possible house purchase in Porthcawl, South Wales. By 5.15 pm it had to be a reviving coffee with brandy.

The day had started by my deciding to launch into the Senior Management Team meeting ('The Future') by tabling a list of my present jobs and expressing grave concern that no time was being found to pass these on. Was my experience and expertise to count for naught? Were those jobs so insignificant that they could be handed on in a twinkling? Of course not. Also I believed, or rather knew, that I had the support of some other members. Clive looked quite taken aback. The agenda immediately became these although I stayed only for the first 20 minutes as lesson one was my last with Year 8 before their exam.

Taught lessons three and four and then sought out three members of the management team to apologise for my hogging the agenda. This was greeted with "about time" and "you are quite right".

Reassured, I was then whisked down to the front garden by Pat where a group of Year 11 Latin students, fresh from their first paper, were present with a standard rose tree which they wanted to help me to plant. Photos were taken and I found it all very moving. There has always been the rumour that Margaret's first name is Rose.

Periods five and six saw more discussion on who picks up what. Some movement but really little result. Clive is to go away and think about a fairer distribution of jobs.

The phone call from a parent – see yesterday – came and I had to ring her back. I launched into all [her son's] misdeeds, thereby stealing thunder.

This was quickly followed by my seeking out [the culprit] from a Year 10 group, one of whom had put itching powder down a failing teacher's back. This happened at 9.45 am and the teacher went home for a bath. She has not reappeared today.

Thursday 13th June 1996

AS I said to Pat [Reid] at 3.30 pm, I could write four sides of A4 about this afternoon and still fail to capture the full account of all this afternoon's events. If I could have filmed or tape-recorded them I could sit down, edit it and then give a fair reflection. Yet so many things happened that I'm sure I have forgotten some already. I suspect I have mentioned before that I think it was Pliny, the Roman writer, who said something about being busy all day yet when asked at the end of it to account for the time he had spent, he found that could be a problem[1].

Taking this afternoon first, the rush began at 1.20 pm when I was asked by Pat to take an assembly. T—— has gone down to the University of Huddersfield and this is going to happen many more times next year. I suspect that it will create friction from those who will have to cover her lessons. I rushed late to this assembly to find the orchestra there ready to perform to Year 8. Year 10, restless and noisy, had also unexpectedly appeared. The deep, stern voice was required which restored calm and in the end everything passed off pleasantly.

Bretton College rang. The external examiner had declared that the student [teacher] we passed very reluctantly she saw as a failure. "Can the decision be rescinded?" Why, why, why didn't I have the courage to say 'fail'? It's no good complaining about the quality of NQTs[2] if the nettle is not grasped during the training period.

Year 10's biggest problem boy was in confrontation with B—— and she said she felt they had almost come to blows. When challenged, tears were shed but he's unmoving and reasoning with him is very difficult.

I was called down to visit the science department where I was met by

P——. Year 7 had been asked to illustrate ways in which we use energy. One bright spark had drawn a couple coupling. More tears and pleas not to send the material to his parents. It had been torn up by the pupil but retrieved by P—— from the waste paper basket, photocopied and a copy was being sent home.

Phone calls from the local paper, pupils' problems with preferences followed.

The morning had been comparatively calm with timetable preparations for next year, some marking, 70 reports to complete for Year 9 and preferences to balance. However, I still felt under great pressure. That's what I shall gladly miss next year: pressure. What a delight it will be to do things in one's own time and at one's own pace.

[1]*Diary entry on 21st March 1996*
[2]*Newly Qualified Teachers*

Friday 14th June 1996

TWO weeks since half term gone already and five to go! After a severe drubbing at badminton last night from Peter Griffin – four games of singles – I was feeling physically exhausted. I thought that this morning I would have felt shattered. As it happened, I have felt quite lively – *mens sana in corpore sano* and all that.

At 8.15 am a father arrived with his daughter who was sporting a black eye. There had been a fight on the bus the previous night. He accepted that his daughter was partly to blame but wanted me to call the two girls together for a big ticking off. I saw the other party later, another girl with an even blacker eye. As so often, [there were] numerous others on the fringe, egging on. It turned out that Clive had had a visit from the second girl's parents at 5.30 pm last night and that the police had become involved.

I should complete this theme by mentioning that at lunchtime 30 'Almondburies'[1], as we call them, were down at school looking for trouble. They had a day off; no such days off in 1961! I phoned the supportive Head of Almondbury High School and then heard that at 3.30 pm a Year 7 pupil had been attacked by some of these same pupils from Almondbury High School. It was said that some had been wielding baseball bats. The victim was taken to hospital in an ambulance. I later discovered that he was the conversation-through-the-hedge boy first mentioned some ten days ago[2]. What a society we live in – atavistic in so many ways and often shades of 'Lord of the Flies'[3].

The other face of school life was on view during the afternoon when the choir, orchestra and soloists, all immaculate despite the heat on what was the hottest day of the year so far, performed beautifully to invited guests in the drama studio. Some of the soloists were good enough to bring a tear to the eye. How very rewarding.

Back to Year 9 Classical Studies lesson early this morning and again a lively and enjoyable one. When asked to suggest differences between Greek and modern schools, the first offering was that we have curtains. True!

Managed a sing at lunchtime but again our fourth member was missing. It again went much better, perhaps [because my] spirits are lifted by the fact that we now appear to have a temporary home in Porthcawl.

Tonight we are going to Clive's for dinner and then tomorrow night Margaret and I will be going to Bradford for a party attended by the former King James's staff who now teach at Greenhead College.

I thought tonight how strange life is going to be without school. Shall I find it empty?

[1] *Pupils of Almondbury High School*

[2] *4th June 1996*

[3] *William Golding's 1954 novel in which a group of schoolboys stranded on an island degenerate into savagery*

Monday 17th June 1996

NOW 24 days to go does begin to sound a very short time. Weekends, perhaps, ought to have been included in my diary for school permeates these too. On Friday we were at Clive's until 1.00 am and on Saturday with ex-KJS staff, now at Greenhead as I mentioned last Friday, until 1.15 am. Inevitably contrasting evenings but both very pleasant although Saturday was more of a chance to unwind.

Today, the best Monday for some time as I seemed to be able to complete lots of small jobs at speed and that does give one a sense of satisfaction. Even small tasks, such as clearing my shelves of all Latin texts and sending them to H——, I saw as a simple but positive act, symbolic of the Approach of the End. The day started with the Senior Management Team trying to sort out next year's roles. This brought one of those jolting moments when it was very clear that D—— and Pat are not always going to see eye-to-eye on many matters and Clive is going to lean in one definite direction. For the last few years we have got along very smoothly but perhaps because we've been an easy three with whom to roll along or to ride over. I forecast stormy waters ahead in '96/'97 but I shall not be on board – I shall have my feet on some sandy shore.

Year 11 had their last GCSE and again what a contrast. Three or four saw it as an opportunity to be unpleasant and even defiant; the majority were delightful and are joining the OAS in record numbers. I was staggered by the rebellious tones of one Year 8 girl and wondered what she'll be like when she is in Year 11.

Management this afternoon until 4.00 pm and making plans for the absence of Clive and P—— in France for four days. It was particularly noticeable today how much I enjoyed the camaraderie and the badinage in the staff room at the end of the school day. This I shall miss enormously.

Tuesday 18th June 1996

023
DAYS TO GO

I SHOULD have mentioned yesterday the failing/failed textiles student [teacher]. I had received a phone call from S—— on Saturday morning forewarning me. The student was at my door by 8.20 am asking about the situation. I had just opened a letter from Bretton which said that she had failed. I ducked out of telling her so early in the day and promised to contact Bretton. I saw her again at break and told her about the fail. Not a pleasant task but I have advised her to think of alternative jobs. I can never see her making a teacher and she should be encouraged to get out now. Later in the day, I received news that she is being allowed to go on to another school in a further attempt to pass her practical teaching.

Briefing this morning, in which I thought afterwards that I'd been too humorous. I was soon brought to earth with a bump. By 9.15 am I was saying, more to myself, that this was a ridiculous situation – I should have been teaching Year 9 Latin but there had been a major fight involving the same two girls as last week. The victim was in a dreadful state with her face puffed up and badly bruised. At the same time a Year 9 boy who was 'on probation' was reported to be wandering the corridors. Typically he denied it until confronted by M—— who had seen him in and out of lessons. The Latin group, therefore, had little effective teaching and I felt they had been cheated.

Half an hour later the police arrived. There were reports of a Year 8 or 9 girl consorting with an Asian bus driver in his bus in our catchment area. 'One of ours?' The description does fit one of our Year 9s, of known bad reputation and strongly believed to be into drugs. The staff were generally very helpful when they saw me under stress. Have I said that Clive and P—— are, of course, in France and that Pat is on a school trip to York?

We had unwelcome visitors in a car around lunchtime but I did manage a sing for 20 minutes which gave me a much needed break. Did Pat's bus duty and then unwound in the staffroom. So welcome!

Wednesday 19th June 1996

I WONDERED once again today if I should adopt a quieter, more resigned approach during these final days but even if I wished to do so, I don't think I could. My style is so much me that I would feel uncomfortable adopting any other and so, I suppose, I shall continue in the present vein until the very last day. Would it be any easier to be relaxed; to turn more blind eyes; to lower the decibel count; to be a weekend rather than a weekday person? I'm sure the answer is 'no' as I would probably have to work much harder at that than at maintaining the present, traditional mode.

Today has been so much better than yesterday. Yet the Year 9 boy who spent five boring hours in isolation yesterday was back on the loose again today by afternoon. I really do feel he is too strange for us to have to deal with in a normal school situation. It's so time-consuming.

It was the last day for the Bretton ITT student teachers and I received kind words, a card and a present from the drama student who was such a problem early on.

I must admit that I have never really felt 100% at ease with my Year 9 Set 3 Classical Studies class. However, at this late stage I feel at last that I am teaching them well. Such a pity that it did not occur earlier. There are more than 30 in the group with a great range of ability but today's lesson seemed to have universal appeal and I left with that little buzz when 70 minutes have passed quite quickly and satisfyingly. It's a real bonus at the end of one's career.

Bus duty and then to a Languages Department meeting. N—— reminded me outside that this was my last ever such meeting. I hadn't realised that but then there are now so many 'last-evers '.

I watched our poor rugby team being hammered by Fartown School; it was like men against little lads. A sad sight before walking home in the pale sunshine.

Thursday 20th June 1996

THE visit to Castleton was supposed to have been my last-ever school trip. But therein lies the danger of saying 'last-ever', for here I was this morning about to go on my 'last-ever' school trip. This time it was with Year 7s to York. I was offered the chance as Year 8 are on exams and so it meant that I would not have to miss any teaching. I had, therefore, happily accepted the invitation.

I am writing this at 9.30 pm, feeling quite drained after 1½ hours of singles badminton with Peter Griffin. Two games all and a very high standard of play. Some tremendous battles and this after an exhausting day at York. Exhausting? Sitting on a coach for four hours? Five teachers and only 45 pupils? These were strident Year 7s and it would have been cruel to have made them sit in silence on the way home. Yet after bumping along at the back of the coach, my ears battered by their shrill voices, I had a real headache and hunger when I finally reached home at 5.00 pm. I do hope that they had a memorable day, for casting my own memory back to school and Sunday School trips some 45 years ago, I do remember them with delight – the highlight of the school year in many ways.

As I've said before, it is so interesting to see how pupils behave in a non-school environment. It's so revealing: characteristics being displayed which one might not see in a year of classroom teaching. The day had been well-planned with worksheets to keep them very busy and only 30 to 40 minutes of free time. The walls, the Minster, picnic on the grass in a chilly wind – and a quiet coffee for staff which was a welcome relief from the constant babble and questioning. It was, I feel, a happy day for all and for me. I'm sure [it was] definitely my last-ever trip!

This close contact with lively young creatures I shall miss but there will be compensations, I hope.

Friday 21st June 1996

ANOTHER Friday evening and we are going out to *The Three Owls* to celebrate the passing of another week or the arrival of the weekend. Four weeks tonight! I can at times feel the tension rising and I shall be mightily relieved when it's all over.

Considering that it was a Friday, and that Clive and P—— are still in France, it passed remarkably smoothly. The fine weather does help for the school is clear at lunchtimes, much steam can be released outside, fewer problems for the LTAs inside and thereby fewer for me.

A note in my tray that a window had been broken by a carelessly kicked football in an area where they are banned. It cost £42 for the glass and the caretakers' time and so meant some Year 10 pupils facing a sizeable bill. L—— pleaded for one boy to be treated sympathetically as he is from a very poor family. When I asked him how much his elaborate hairstyle cost he informed me that it was £10. Priorities!

Year 9 Classical Studies passed easily after a slow first 15 minutes as it took me that time to get into my stride.

A phone call from a parent regarding a letter telling her her daughter would begin a limited GCSE course next year. She will be taking only six subjects as she is one of the weakest in the year. The mother clearly had not understood the letter and thought she would not be taking any. "You see, Mr Bush, she wants to be a lawyer."

Another phone call, this time internal, from W——. "Four boys are impersonating sheep." I didn't query his use of 'impersonating' on semantic grounds but I was annoyed that after 20 years of teaching his [class] discipline is no better than when he started. This is such a pity for he is a most generous man, kind hearted and very well read. He's also a great conversationalist with strong views on a wide range of subjects.

Marked some Year 8 Latin papers. Some are excellent, others dreadfully weak. Poorly taught? Too difficult an exam? Lazy revision? Less able children? Mostly the latter I feel, for the general view is that this year is intrinsically less able. But why? This has always intrigued me, for with 170 pupils in any one year their ability should average out to be the same as any other year.

The week finished on an annoying note, for three girls had been found in the boys' toilets and damage had been done. All denied doing any damage but then how serious an offence is it? I'll see Clive on Monday when he returns. He'll have quite a flurry of decisions to make.

Monday 24th June 1996

NINETEEN days to go, so now into the teens. A feeling of increasing tension pervades although offset tonight by a 5.30 pm run, shower and salad tea on the patio in the sun. The weekend had been an emotional one, for Margaret and I cleared the loft and mutually decided to burn the past ie all our letters, diaries etc. Much of daughter Catherine's childhood stuff was taken to the tip.

Added to this I marked 60 Year 8 Latin papers, some excellent, some – far too many – dreadfully weak with obviously little attempt to revise prepared work. This led to a discussion in the staff room during the morning break when a group of us – and not all oldies – agreed that pupils generally are far too laid-back, have lost the will or the ability to study really hard. It may be that they have never been taught or trained to do so. So much is spoon-fed to them. Both A—— and I agreed that the modern Year 11 GCSE student could not begin to tackle a 1960s GCE paper and Margaret fully agrees with regard to Spanish. I know the approach is different today but as far as difficulty goes I would defy anyone to prove that today's papers are not far easier.

Clive and P —— [are] back from France and had enjoyed their experience.

Pat and I had both registered a degree of 'mission-not-fully-accomplished': we were waiting for Clive's resumé of 'The Big Breakthrough' but it was not forthcoming.

There were certainly plenty of mundane matters for him to pick up during our summary of the last few days of last week. But I was grateful for his thanking us for keeping things running smoothly. How a bit of positive stroking helps at every level.

Had to smile when Lesley from the kitchen reported that if there is any problem in the local Co-op, the manageress threatens to ring Mr Bush. We have never met. What will it be like to be Mr Unknown?

Tuesday 25th June 1996

A GLORIOUSLY sunny day and, dare I say, one of the most inactive for some considerable time. What a contrast to one week ago. The walk to school was delightful, a true summer morning when I furtively performed my annual civic duty of cutting back briars and branches crossing or overhanging the paths I have now trodden for 12 years. Unless somebody does the same, the paths will be overgrown and impassable within three years.

Year 9 Latin was most enjoyable for me and I hope for them, a lesson with a liberal helping of etymological offerings. They do seem to feed happily on these and I hope it isn't self-delusion.

Did some stripping of my study's festooned walls and shredding of accumulated piles of paper on my desk. I wonder what percentage increase there has been in paper used today compared with that in 1961. In the days of the 'Banda'[1] or whatever it was called and later Gestetner[2] duplicating machines – themselves a real novelty – comparatively little paper was produced. Now whole forests are used up. I suppose it helps with the smooth running of day- to-day school life.

I am still going over Preferences while C—— and L—— are working on the timetable all harmoniously in my room. This occupied most of the rest of the day. Contrast this with a growing dispute between R—— and T—— over the staffing of PSE[3]. Two very strong willed people here and neither, it seems, is willing to compromise. It eventually may be for Clive to adjudicate but he's already, predictably stated that R—— will have to teach what he's been allocated. I can see trouble aplenty next year and Pat has the same sentiments.

So often I seem to have been the typical deputy, the buffer, the go-between, the peacemaker. Who said "The successful head wears a frown on his deputy's face?"[4] and who is going to fill that calming role? But there I go again, predicting my own indispensability.

The school will certainly roll on and I'll be a yesterday's man.

[1] *Spirit duplicators patented by Block & Anderson, in widespread use in the 1950s*
[2] *Duplicators invented by Hungarian David Gestetner using wax stencils, widely used from the 1960s to the 1980s*
[3] *Personal and Social Education*
[4] *David Bush, 1996*

Wednesday 26th June 1996

IF yesterday was an 'easy' day today has been 'difficult'. I had that tight feeling this morning which I haven't had for some time. Why? Simply because there were so many tasks to complete and people to see.

I returned one Year 8 Latin group's exam papers and, as mentioned before, I marked them last weekend and found many disappointing. I tried not to be too hard but I gave them a homily on the importance of revision and concentration. I hope it will sow a few seeds. I did tell them how during a period of exam revision my mother used to persuade me to put my light out and I agreed only on the condition that she woke me at 6.30 the following morning so I could continue. This was not too hard on her as my father left for work at 6.45 am! The pupils looked stunned.

Periods 3 and 4 Classical Studies were covered by A—— and F—— as it was a Senior Management Team meeting mainly to allocate jobs. I feel that there is some unfair unloading being done and forecast that there will be some unwilling recipients. We are now to go away, think about it and report back. At least there is progress at last although I suppose nothing is yet finalised and won't be until next week.

It's just like our house sale. I rang our solicitor, who of course is an Old Almondburian, and he informed me that no contracts have yet been exchanged although originally it had been suggested that this would happen 2½ weeks ago. It hangs over me. Now I am told that it will happen tomorrow. These are wearying days – I shall be pleased when they are over.

There were some compensations in the form of cards, such as the one received from the USA. This was from one of my former outstanding students who is now a teacher there and for whom I was his "model and inspiration". It makes me feel humble, proud and yes – it makes it all seem worthwhile.

I was at Greenhead College to fulfil an invitation to have lunch with some of the staff there. More pleasant words exchanged. It's not wise to drink sherry, eat too much strawberry gateau and then hope to be at one's productive best during the afternoon.

Thursday 27th June 1996

I NEARLY always wait to accompany Clive to Briefing. This morning I went in ahead of him and then was asked to leave. Obviously they were discussing my departure. I sat in my room feeling strangely isolated. I know that it was necessary but I did feel rather uncomfortable.

Reciprocated a cover which M—— did for me yesterday. Then an extended break before Sports Day track events. [But] the highlight of the morning was not connected with athletics for it had to be our secretary appearing on the horizon. From a distance, I could see she had a piece of paper in her hand. I guessed it was for me and that it was from our solicitor ringing to say contracts had been exchanged. I was correct on both counts. A great feeling of relief caused me to view my last sports day in an even rosier light.

It was a lovely sunny morning. As details of the new house in Porthcawl had arrived by this morning's post, I felt even more that this chapter of life was moving rapidly to an end. The behaviour of pupils and the atmosphere were generally very good – better, I felt, than for some time. C—— and L—— were not present on the field but [were] up in my room

196

timetabling. As I sat nearby this afternoon watching their expertise and greatly admiring it, for the first time I really felt an outsider, left behind by modern technology. Those times of working with pencil and rubber for days, nights and weekends and of agonising over compiling the timetable seem like something from the last century. Yet such methods were being used until quite recently.

The day finished, as often, with an up and down or rather the reverse. The down was that somebody spat on D—— from an upper bus window – to be investigated tomorrow – and then our quartet had a superb 25 minute burst. I shall miss them and it.

Friday 28th June 1996

ONLY three more weeks to go. I shall be ready! Am I trying to convince myself or is it a genuine feeling? It was coffee and brandy time on returning home this evening at the end of a demanding day.

Last night it had been the annual staff car rally organised by Peter Griffin, his wife, Liz and us. It saw the best turnout for some years and concluded at the YMCA. The convivial atmosphere was a delight to witness. To see those who a few hours before had been discussing the vicissitudes of school life and [who] were now completely relaxed, roaring with laughter and indulging in wit and repartee made the hours of preparation so worthwhile.

Yet it meant an after-midnight bedtime and being awoken, prematurely according to my body, at 6.40 am. Add to this the fact that it was pouring with rain and I arrived at school feeling very wet. Not a good start to a Friday morning. This was exacerbated by my mentioning to Clive the spitting incident from last night. His only comment: "There is a message here for the staff – don't get too near the buses." I couldn't believe my ears and he could tell I was upset. He's probably right but not a very discreet remark. I'm sure he wouldn't have said that in the staffroom, or at least I hope not.

One boy was seen spitting but it's unclear exactly when – and he is emotionally disturbed. He is still seeing the school psychiatrist so even if he were guilty I don't think we would gain much by punishing him.

Year 9 Classical Studies saw a hesitant start but eventually was fine. Another highlight of the day was the organisation of the staff (teaching and ancillary) photo. The doubtful weather meant that it was uncertain if the photograph would be taken inside or out. It improved sufficiently for it to be taken outside – fittingly on the lawn in front of the old school house. It was amazing how suddenly everyone (with the exception of F—— who declined to join us) appeared as if by magic.

C—— and L—— continue the '96/'97 timetabling while I began the great lustration[1] of my main filing cabinet. Not strictly a *lustrum* as there must have been 20+ years' accumulation of material therein. A ruthless attack produced piles and piles of paper. A satisfying way to finish the week but an emotional one too.

[1]*A clearing out, from the ancient Greek and ancient Roman purification ceremony* Lustratio

CHAPTER 11

July
1996

Welcome To

DURKER ROODS
— HOTEL —

84 851413

The final month begins

Monday 1st July 1996

THE final month, the last three weeks. Dinner at Jack's [Taylor] on Saturday and on Sunday I was at *The Jungle*[1] with five colleagues and friends and families. The latter visit was to 'complete my education before migrating to the south-west.' This was a rugby league match between Castleford and Halifax.

Back to the reality of school this morning. A cold, wet, November-like day. A pity, for walking to school through the fields on a summer's morning will remain as one of my most treasured memories. The day did not begin well with news of at least four staff off including two senior. This inevitably meant more problems coming my way.

Despite that fear, it has not been too demanding a day. A smile left over from Friday. We read that 'Greek athletes received woollen jerkins and pitchers of oil as prizes.' "Do you understand what this means?" I asked pupil J——. "Yes, Sir, they got some oil paintings."

Spent at least another hour this morning going through my files. As before they contain so many memories, courses going back some years, initiatives which came to naught, others which bore fruit, references for colleagues/pupils who have gone on to high positions – and above all dozens of letters from the last 20+ years. I am amazed at how many there are. There must be at least a dozen from Gorden Kaye alone. I hadn't the courage to dispose of all at one go so I'm sure I shall sift, save and re-read when in my metaphorical rocking chair.

The investigation into the spitting from the bus continues with more supergrasses emerging. Pupil P—— admits to flicking a chewed-up bus ticket out of the window. I suspect he spat but it is going to be very difficult to prove.

Management curtailed because of Pat's absence and Clive's need to 'catch up'. That man is putting himself under increased pressure and, I feel, looks as though he is becoming ill. I have to survive 14 days, he has five years.

[1] *The Wheldon Road ground of Castleford Tigers Rugby League Club in Castleford, West Yorkshire*

Tuesday 2nd July 1996

STILL another 13 days to go and I shall soon have finished clearing my room. This afternoon I reached [filing cabinet] pocket number 86. Carried the last bucket of paper down to the bin in the Old Kitchen Yard. I had earlier taken a huge pile of references down to the secretary for shredding over the next few days. Inevitably, I read some [references] and they aroused memories of successes and disappointments. My role as ITT coordinator has meant an enormous increase in the number required over recent years. [A pile of] examination analyses was similarly bulky, and D—— requested it so that he could see, as examinations officer, if he lacked any.

The *Huddersfield Examiner* rang to fix an interview for the final week. This will not be easy and I shall have to be on good form.

Lessons 1 and 2 of Year 9 Latin were not as sparkling as I would normally expect. Are we all getting tired at the end of a tiring academic year?

Senior Management Team followed for one hour; very frustrating again, for attempts to be thoroughly democratic mean that the whole business is becoming very protracted; so much so that few final decisions are being taken and more meetings are needed. 'He died of a surfeit of paper and meetings' – an epitaph for a teacher.

At the end of school I had a frank 20 minutes with Clive conveying some of the SMT's concerns. I tried to explain diplomatically that some are reluctant to speak up as they fear being verbally bowled over or out for a duck. (What a clumsy attempt at a cricketing metaphor!)

Wednesday 3rd July 1996

LAST night was my last ever OAS Executive [Meeting] and it turned out to be a very tame affair. Attendance was thin and the controversial Trust Fund saga[1] was over in three minutes without any real progress being made or reported.

Yet I fear it will run for some time and could yet cause a major division between the School and the Society, a schism which would cause me great personal sadness. Jack spoke at some length about my service to the Society and the enormous increase in membership since I became involved. Very moving words. And yet, in a simple way and perhaps more moving, was the exchange with Norman Kerrod, editor of the newsletter, whom I have known peripherally for many years. Simple handshake, words of farewell and of thanks and we parted company.

At 9.15 pm on my returning home Margaret said that D—— had rung and he needed to contact Clive over a crisis. This set me worrying and I took my first *Nytol* for some time. I was in to see D—— first thing this morning. 'Crisis' was somewhat of an exaggeration but he feels great concern over the lack of positive teaching being done by A——, a member of his department. Subsequently, there have been complaints from parents and the question arises again how to sack a non-performing teacher. Virtually impossible and what a disgrace that it should be so and how unfair on the pupils.

I was telephoned earlier by a parent whose daughter has gone missing, one whom I saw yesterday. She has changed dramatically in a year; from being pleasant and cheerful she has become awkward and rebellious. In Year 9 Classical Studies group, there is another girl with even greater problems – bigger than we can deal with. She is bright but even for Jack and for me she is virtually refusing to do anything. I don't remember such a rebellious attitude in 35 years of teaching.

Off to the Swimming Gala at Cambridge Road Baths. Jack is having a training day (at his age, as he says!) so I took over the announcements. What a noise! There has always been noise at the Gala but [the pupils] could not be fully quietened even for the start of each race. They are so conditioned by TV programmes to shout throughout.

Popped into town and signed up for the house in Porthcawl.
[1]*See 3rd June 1996*

Thursday 4th July 1996

THERE have been so many invitations to dinner recently that we went to the Griffins for the last time last night. Not ideal being midweek but we do enjoy their company so much; Peter and I occupy similar positions in that we are both deputies at Greenhead

College and KJS respectively while our wives have, in the past, both taught in the same languages department at Huddersfield Technical College. For many years now we have had these cathartic sessions which have been so much valued and which we shall miss enormously. It was after midnight before we were home and a disturbed night followed after such richness of food, wine and conversation. It was not surprising then that I was not in the best of form first thing – most unfortunate in a way as we had Year 6, i.e. next year's new Year 7, visiting today.

B—— introduced me to his group and yes, they had heard of me and knew I should not be seeing them in September. I don't know who was happier or more relieved. It also meant my taking K——'s lesson as he is a Year 7 tutor in '96/'97.

This meant a double lesson for Year 8. After a return of their Latin exam papers I decided that was enough formal teaching and I offered them some light relief. They listened intently as I reflected on yesterday's Swimming Gala. I explained how much the event had changed from the Boys' Grammar School days when disqualifications were common for the slightest infringement of rules, its cups for individual races and the formal presentation to the Swimming Captain of the winning house of a large trophy. This was always presented by the chairman of the Old Almondburians' [Society]. Yesterday's event was enjoyable but more of a 'fun' day. It has lost the discipline involved and that's a serious loss in my opinion. There is plenty of 'fun' outside school. Why does everything have to be 'fun' or is this just one more example of how out of touch I am?

The timetable is not going well, so it was time for my intervention and for explaining to heads of department that they cannot have matters exactly as they requested. I suspect they think we haven't tried hard enough when in fact the reverse is often the case.

All gearing up now for tomorrow night's European Evening and we managed half an hour's practice this afternoon during period 7. I think I have seen Clive for only two minutes today, which must be a record. Feeling weary at the end of the day so I went home early.

Friday 5th July 1996

FRIDAY again! Doesn't it come round! A very trite expression admittedly but nevertheless so very true. Two weeks tonight – it all sounds very imminent, and then? Shall I be able to turn off, turn away, turn down an invitation to return? Today, for example, a new appointment was made and I can see many problems arising from it. I felt quite upset and somewhat annoyed that I had not, contrary to normal practice, been consulted or involved. And then I thought that it would not affect me in the slightest. I reflected that it is still my school and then countered that by adding that it would not be after August. I told myself that I would still retain an interest and feel concern. And so the internal dilemma rages. I do hope I shall be able to make a clean start in Porthcawl and forget so much about The School.

The girl who ran away and caused a police search has returned. The mother asked for a low-key approach from the staff. The girl was revelling in her notoriety by registration at 8.45 am and by second lesson was refusing to move when requested. This is a pupil aged 12/13 and we wonder what a problem she will be when she is 16. And Pat tells me of a pupil aged 13 who is to go on the pill. What a state we have reached! Where is the innocence, where are the simple pleasures of childhood? But then, what is childhood?

Year 9 Classical Studies was, as before, initially hard work after a sound *Nytol*-assisted sleep but eventually we were into the swing of ancient Greek sports.

L—— failed to appear for our quartet practice.

In period 1 I did some cover for a supply Maths teacher. We have moved him on to classes where he is less of an embarrassment. It would be better to pay him to stay at home and teach via remote control!

Managed 15 minutes' singing practice at lunchtime and completed a few reports. The space allocated to each subject means that anything fewer than 20 words seems skimped or inadequate. A far cry from the 'satisfactory' and 'must try harder' of yesteryear.

Tonight is the European Evening and our quartet will be singing in ten different languages in one item. The audience will be invited to write down which language we are using. Should be fun.

Monday 8th July 1996

NOW it's into single figures and the tension is rising. Last night I was seized quite suddenly with waves of apprehension which left me unable to get to sleep – rare for me – and still awake at 1.30 am. *Nytol* taken which resulted in the inevitable short-of-sleep, drugged feeling at 6.40 am. This didn't leave me until later in the day.

In fact, for the first hour I did little apart from feel guilty and reflect on what I am going to say at Friday night's Dinner. It was around 10.00 am before I began to feel in a workmanlike mood and after a slow beginning the day took on its own pace.

Management meeting during periods five and six. There are a number of matters I feel strongly about but I've decided to leave quietly. I don't want to create unnecessary ill-feeling at this stage and I'm sure others feel the same. It may well be that they would also disagree strongly but for me it's 'rock my cradle, not my boat' time –a motto I thought up a year ago and decided to put on my door when my departure became general knowledge. Yet I never got round to it.

I do see the cracks already appearing in the new Senior Management Team – or is it that the present one has been particularly harmonious, or subservient? Do cracks simply mean opportunities for 'wide-ranging discussions'? Shall I find out? Shall I care?

A retirement card from the two couples across the road from the school entrance was particularly touching. Big Tree is alive. Long live Big Tree! Mr Skeratt, arboriculturist, arrived this afternoon at 4.30 pm by appointment, following up the visit on 8th February. He declared Big Tree in general to be in good health and in need only of a little lopping. He'll send a full report but this was a great relief. A delightful man, dropped me off at Foxglove Road and a day that did not begin particularly well ended happily.

Tuesday 9th July 1996

A MUCH better, assisted night's sleep but tonight I again began to feel rather tired despite, on reflection, the day not having been particularly busy or stressful. Or was it? I feel in such a perpetual state of tension that superficially I sense I am above it but in reality I am probably suffering.

Year 9 Latin this morning was almost certainly the last lesson with them. Next week it's house cricket and rounders unless of course it rains which makes all things rather uncertain. Yet I had to presume it was the final lesson. Not a particular dynamic one and that's a pity, for they are almost without exception a delightful group. I did leave the last five minutes for goodbyes, "thank yous" from me and a stirring "Vale, Magister!"from them. One boy whispered "thank you"as he left.

The two timetablers C—— and L—— were struggling away in my room and after I had completed my last set of reports – I wrote on Laura Whiteley's words to the effect, 'This is my very last report at KJS. Preserve it! It may become a collectors' item'. I suddenly felt quite superfluous and for 10 minutes I walked the lonely corridors.

The Greenhead College librarian came this afternoon to discuss the possible removal of the Taylor Dyson Library to her institution. I must mention that during the Big Clear Out I discovered the detention book from 1972 onwards. It's quite hilarious in parts, especially as son Alan's name appears not infrequently. The offences which merited an ASD (After School Detention) in those days would for the most part be considered trivial today. The detention room would be packed to overflowing every night if the same sanctions still applied. But then that was the grammar school and today's institution is so very different. Simply put we are not comparing like with like.

Jack and I discussed the minutes books of the Philatelic and the Scientific Societies. How immaculate they appear, how impressive. It's such a pity that today there are no such clubs in KJS. How much we feel we have lost. However, others would argue that other worthwhile activities have replaced them.

Took a last-minute assembly and used my baked beans tin theme. I realise this needs an explanation. On one occasion, I went to an assembly with no prepared theme but managed to produce one at the last minute. When I told a colleague about this she said that I should never worry for I could produce a theme from a baked beans tin label. To prove her correct I took the said label into my next assembly and worked out a message from it to those ranged before me.

Wednesday 10th July 1996

THAT 7 doesn't look very big. Only seven days left after today! Despite the nearness of the end I feel better today. More sound sleep has helped but otherwise not easy to discover why that should be.

I had my last lesson – weather permitting – with Year 8 Latin (German Set) and Year 9 Classical Studies. The former was really a normal lesson apart from the parting words: had another rousing, "Valete, discipuli!" "Vale, Magister!".

Year 9 Classical Studies turned into an hour's quiz. It may have been only the brighter ones who were producing the answers but I was pleasantly surprised at how much they knew i.e. how much they have learned about the classical world in just one double lesson per week. That's gratifying.

Break and another moving moment. Retirement cards arriving which included Little Miss Nose Stud who came to my room clutching, somewhat sheepishly, an envelope. I opened it. A lovely 'thank you' card and a sweet smile. I was very touched and I think she saw the tears in my eyes. What are her real feelings, I wonder? How much influence we teachers have. What power! I still find it frightening and humiliating in so many ways.

There has been a breakthrough on the timetable by way of a compromise. Although I will be giving it the nod, M—— and C—— are doing all the hard work.

At the Parents' AGM[1] last night the Science Department's problems were highlighted. Another very heavy burden for Clive to carry and in a cowardly way I am relieved that I shall not have to share any of it.

Bus duty was followed by the staff tennis tournament. More than 20 people playing in a most convivial atmosphere with much laughter. Now that is something I shall miss ...if it is not replaced.

[1]*An independent organisation of pupils' parents with its own committee, set up to organise events and discuss any topics considered relevant to the education and general welfare of their children*

Thursday 11th July 1996

TRYING very hard to keep calm, take things easy, not to ruffle feathers, to distance myself from decisions which will have no effect on me. But it's far from easy. There are aspects of 'Policy for '96/'97' with which I do not agree and decisions about reducing certain colleagues' timetables to enable them to do more non-teaching jobs which I think are unfair or unnecessary ...but I remain silent. The amount of time that is now spent outside the classroom is enormous. Is it really so essential? We have lost sight of the teaching wood for the Inset trees.

Many of these thoughts were provoked by the Senior Management Team meeting this morning when it became clear that not all my tasks will be re-allocated this term. Possibly taught my last-ever Latin lesson and I hadn't realised that until later in the day. Still that was probably a good thing.

More retirement cards including a delightful one from Year 9 Latin group. I took a phone call from the Kirkheaton primary and junior school head. I am his regular contact when our pupils have been a nuisance on his premises. Kind words were again expressed about my help and best wishes sent for retirement.

Sat down with B—— for 20 minutes. Another pouring out of concerns. Colleagues seem to be unburdening themselves while I'm still around.

A knife incident took up much time. A Year 7 had brought a kitchen knife into school which had "fallen into his bag in the kitchen and remained unnoticed." I could not get a straight story. Another pupil had been cut with this same knife. Not a serious injury but nevertheless it needed a ruthless follow-up. A supportive father came in and his son and knife were removed.

Friday 12th July 1996

I SHALL be greatly relieved when today is over, for although it's now 5.30 pm, the best or worst is yet to come! Tonight is the dinner at the *Durker Roods Hotel*[1] at Meltham, being held to celebrate my retirement, with 85 people present. I know it's all going to be very emotional and I shall be making a speech of thanks. I have ideas mapped out but as usual I shall speak without notes. I just hope everyone enjoys a memorable evening.

All this is about 'self' when today at around lunchtime Margaret's retirement began. Greenhead College finished at lunchtime so in the retirement stakes she's a full week ahead of me and she too will be pleased when it's tomorrow. She has never liked 'being on show'.

At school, I indulged myself by teaching Year 9 bottom set a little Latin which they seemed to enjoy and then it was back to the timetable, ironing out the final wrinkles. I was interrupted by the arrival of the father of the boy who was 'stabbed' yesterday. He was not concerned about the incident but wished to protest loudly about nobody contacting him at home last night to find out how his son was. I explained that Clive was dealing with the matter and I knew he had had a very busy evening. I think I placated him. The offender is to be suspended and will have a visit from the police. I was so busy that I forgot for the first time to go to a singing practice period six. Unwelcome visitors at lunchtime and the police sent for but generally a relaxed atmosphere in glorious sunshine.

Lots more retirement cards, a very kind letter from staff colleague S—— and even a bottle of brandy and a card from the West Indian lady who cleans my room and whom I see only infrequently.

Then while [I was] trying to unwind a little at home, Clive rang to protest over Graham Cliffe's letter in the Old Almondburians' Society newsletter. He is threatening to resign his presidency. What timing! Could he not have waited until Monday?

Addendum

I'm breaking with nearly a year's convention by adding a note about last night's celebratory dinner at the *Durker Roods Hotel*. It was indeed a wonderful occasion. 85 people present on a lovely summer's evening. The guests ranged from Fran, the new office girl, to people such as Francis Bareham and Peter Heywood from the early '60s. At the entrance lobby, Margaret and I greeted all our guests assisted by our wonderful master of ceremonies, Jack, and his wife. At 7.30 pm precisely, we were applauded into the dining room and made our way to the top table. The meal was excellent with singing by our quartet between courses and I received a beautifully inscribed pewter tankard from the other three members. There were speeches by Jack and Clive and the presentation of a very expensive camcorder as a parting gift. My speech, [which I had] thought about at length but delivered as planned without notes, was well received and I was most touched by a prolonged, standing ovation. Opportunities then for more intimate exchanges which went on until midnight.

A memorable night indeed!

[1] *Hotel in Meltham near Huddersfield, originally built in the 1870s as a large private residence and the home of David Brown of David Brown Ltd in the 1970s. A 'rood' is historically a measure of land area equal to a quarter of an acre.*

Monday 15th July 1996

THE final week and the last lap, the run in – whatever sporting metaphor is chosen, the tape is in sight. Having taken most of the weekend to recover both physically and emotionally from the drama on Friday night, it was helpful to walk to school on a lovely summer morning, having left Margaret in bed to enjoy the first day of her retirement.

It was strange walking into the staffroom and seeing colleagues whom I last saw some 60 hours previously in a totally different environment. Inevitably, comments were passed about the success of Friday evening, but as usual the everyday bustle of school life, with Year 10 back after work experience, soon took over. As for myself, I had resolved to try very hard to keep calm, not to become too involved or emotional and, if possible, not to issue reprimands to anyone for having their shirt out, two earrings, wearing trainers, loud behaviour and the like – not easy for one, who according to Margaret, finds it physically impossible to turn a blind eye. I was not 100% successful but surprised myself by how close I came. All in all, it has been a comparatively easy day and at 4.00 pm I felt surprisingly relaxed.

The schism between the chairman and president of the OAS over the trust fund causes me considerable angst, but otherwise people have been very kind.

I was particularly moved by a phone call from Ken Leech in Melbourne, Australia at 9.30 am wishing me a happy final week and retirement. I do hope we get to Australia to meet him and his wife[1]. Home for a coffee and cake on the terrace – now that's what I'm looking forward to enjoying regularly.

Should have mentioned that today saw my last Jessop House assembly, my beloved House which never achieved winning the Champion Trophy in my 36 years at the school. They did give me three hearty cheers as I left.
[1]*DAB visited Australia with grand-daughter Anna in 2012 (see also 23rd May 1996)*

Tuesday 16th July 1996

AND then there were three! What stands out in my mind today? More cards and presents, The *Huddersfield Examiner* and a glorious summer day with cricket and rounders house matches on our idyllic fields. They last over two days only now, whereas in the '60s it seemed that the last week or more was all cricket with seniors, middle and juniors. Today I was impressed by the turnout of the cricketers and the amount of kit they carried. Even the young ones seem to be carrying coffin-like bags for all their gear. Anyone with his own bat in the '60s was regarded with awe.

More cards and small, touching presents from Years 8 and 9 pupils and a beautiful Latin-inscribed plate from Patrick O'Brien and his wife. The *Huddersfield Examiner* photographer had me pose before the school sign and Roger L'Amie brought me video copies of last Friday's celebration dinner. Patrick and Dave Bradford had insisted I join them for a pub lunch in the *Rose and Crown*. Margaret joined us and what a pleasant break it was. That must be the first lunchtime out for many, many years – and I enjoyed it – and I didn't feel guilty!

Timetables have been given out today and inevitably there were the usual moans and groans but no major disasters. No praise so far; there is usually somebody who passes a compliment. I didn't mention the Senior Management Team meeting during periods one and two which saw quite a lot of business rapidly transacted. What a change! But time is now at a premium.

Wednesday 17th July 1996

THE antepenultimate! And generally a happy one. There had been a very long and controversial Governors' meeting last night but although normally the main issues would have concerned me directly, I felt I could nor should any longer exercise influence. Instead I was determined to enjoy the day. Again, gloriously sunny and becoming hot. More cricket and rounders on the fields and, glory be, Jessop, (my house, although senior staff are supposed to be neutral) won the Cricket Cup this afternoon for the first time in many, many years. It was a triumphant note on which to finish house sport in which I have had such a keen interest for so many years. There is no doubt that the system is still well worthwhile with spirits high and competition keen.

The day began with more cards from pupils, little presents, a letter from a grateful parent and a bottle of wine from a Year 11 Latin student. "But I've had my present from the Latin group!" "Yes, but this is from me!"

This could be one gigantic ego trip if I'm not careful. At lunchtime, the dinner ladies' presentation took place . This was really something. Photos, speeches and gifts took some 25 minutes. Chocolates, wine, fluffy banana – in-joke– and six beautiful, cut glass red wine glasses. I even had a special visit from dentist, Philip Shaw[1], a 1971 leaver and with whom I've had so many enjoyable games of football. His card said 'very firm but very fair'. In many ways I would be happy to have that as my epitaph.

The timetable is still causing minor problems but generally has been accepted. Another masterpiece but that's what the timetablers say every year.

My very last bus duty was carried out in the afternoon heat. The pupils seemed almost soporose. What a contrast to last year with delayed buses in pouring rain. Then off to the music practice room where the quartet is attempting to video and record all the songs they have sung over the last five years.

[1]Philip Shaw attended King James's Grammar School from 1964-71. He studied dentistry at the University of Liverpool and for many years was the Huddersfield Town Football Club dentist.

Thursday 18th July 1996

THE penultimate! Having just telephoned three removal firms for estimates, the imminence of tomorrow and goodbye teaching and Huddersfield are emphasised still further. I am surprising myself by how comparatively calm I feel. Again, surprisingly, I am sleeping unaided very soundly and this is helping, as too is the weather. Hotter by the day and forecast to continue right over our open house weekend. This means [that] half an hour with a drink, the *Daily Telegraph* crossword and a relaxing chair on the patio all greatly speed up the unwind after school.

Today? As yesterday, abiding impression is pupils coming to my door with cards and gifts. Jack there with wine and card before school, his card beautifully worded. The lunchtime supervisors presented me with a paperweight etched with school crest and kind words, kisses and photographs.

While all this was going on HM Ofsted inspector was making his preliminary visit to KJS – lasting three hours – before the full inspection next November. Did I feel a twinge of guilt or was that a smug smile? More of the latter, I think, though I also feel for colleagues with the extra pressure now imposed.

Today also saw the last assembly I shall take if not attend. [It was] thanks to Clive and Pat who thoughtfully had invited me to take this one, as it was centred around the presentation of six trophies for House events. I'm afraid I really enjoyed it – a bit of self indulgence (not over the top I hope) but an opportunity to laud our House system and all the competition it brings being, as I said, very competitive by nature myself. Read my two favourite prayers and went out to loud applause.

What will it be like tomorrow?

Friday 19th July 1996

Das Ende. La fin. El fin. Finis. The End. In any language, that's it then! I have been unable to pick up my pen until beyond 7.00 pm, having felt so emotionally drained that it is only now that I can bring myself so to do. And I know I shall find it impossible to describe adequately my feelings, as they are so diverse and – predictably – I feel almost numb. Yet if I left writing until much later or until the calmer hours of tomorrow, would I still be able to capture the spirit of today? Shall I have time? And will it be calmer, for tomorrow and on Sunday it is Open House at Foxglove Road when a lot of people are expected?

Overriding impression? Was it okay? Did I let myself or the school down in anyway? Should I have done this, said that? It would have been better if... and it's all too late now. Accept it. It's finished. There is no repeat performance. People say that it was a great day and I should be happy it's over and that it has gone well.

Another beautiful walk to school. Every day I regularly see the same people walking their dog or going to work and to these I say "Good morning". Today when I added "And goodbye" they replied, "We know; we know who you are." Humbling and amazing.

One of the most poignant moments of the whole

day occurred as I arrived at the Old Kitchen Entrance. For there to welcome me was my dear friend and colleague over the last 35 years, Jack. He greeted me with his so-firm handshake and wished me well for this, my final day.

During the morning there was a succession of presents, cards and tears at my door. My very last lesson was, in theory, Classical Studies with that lovely, small Set 6 group. In practice, I simply talked about my 35 years at King James's School and all the changes I had seen. They listened intently.

There was a fax from Australia at lunchtime and a large card from the staff – and so to my final assembly. Clive was unable to be there as he was visiting his wife in hospital (but, much relief, the prognosis is good). In his absence, Pat took the assembly with her usual calm efficiency. A presentation from the school was made of a series of VHS bird videos.

In my final speech, I think I described myself as a kind of dark chocolate: hard on the outside but with a very soft centre. I received a standing ovation on entry and on departure. To say I was very moved is an understatement. I waved to the whole school and to the kitchen ladies lined up on the balcony of the sports hall.

And so I left and the next phase of life can now begin.

RETIREMENT

2nd September
1996

Today is the first day of the new term and here I am, with Margaret, looking down at our 3-day-old granddaughter, Anna. Nearby are the golden sands and the sparkling sea of Porthcawl on the south coast of Wales. I feel relaxed and content – no more tightness under the ribs. This is what retirement is all about.

And it's my birthday.

AFTERWORD

ANYONE taking a trip down to St Helen's Gate in Almondbury, or looking across the valley from Farnley Line, will see that King James's School is still standing. Despite my hubristic forecast that with my departure in 1996, and that of other senior colleagues the following year, the school would fall down or at least fall apart, this has proved completely unfounded. Indeed, the school has thrived beyond all expectations.

Under the admirable stewardship of Robert Lamb and his successor, the present Principal Ian Rimmer, King James's continues to achieve outstanding examination results and is vastly oversubscribed. The imminent closure of Almondbury High School will see more building on the site and an expansion to approaching 1,000 pupils.

The rift between School and Old Almondburians' Society, which caused me so much anxiety in my final year, is no more. Relations between the two bodies have never been stronger. The persistence of the Old Almondburians' Society in pursuing Kirklees Council for maladministration of the school's ancient trusts resulted in a six- figure settlement which provides the school with a welcome annual income of thousands of pounds.

King James's achieved Special Science School status in 2004, celebrated its 400th anniversary in fine style in 2008 and became an academy in 2012.

The demise of Latin in the school is a personal regret, as was the surprise felling of Big Tree the year after my retirement despite the reassurances from the tree surgeon that it was generally in 'good health'. The fall of Big Tree did however leave space for a new science laboratory to be erected. I should add at this juncture that my precious Year 11 Latin group did achieve outstanding results, although not 100% success; there were two Ds!

I had vowed never to enter the school again, once I had left in July 1996. Yet I did attend Old Almondburians' Society dinners held in the drama studio. Eventually, I succumbed and was given a guided tour of the school by Patrick O'Brien. What a transformation! What had been rather dull and gloomy areas of the school had been transformed. Now it was positively bursting with light and excellent display boards. 'My room' now resembled Mission Control.

And what about me? Time's inexorable march has had some effects but I've really enjoyed an idyllic retirement. Nearly 25 years on, it is strange to think that those Year 8 pupils are now 36 years old, and Year 11 pupils are approaching 40. Little Miss Nose Stud will be 37 and perhaps will have a family of her own, all with nose studs. I should love to know.

Perhaps our wonderful OAS will unearth more stories, more contacts. Who knows? Could this lead to a sequel? Certainly, I could fill it with details of how I have spent my very fulfilling retirement. Helping to bring up two grandchildren dominated the early years although all that family has now left to live in London and with Alan and wife, Jane, living in the Cotswolds, we have no relations within 100 miles.

I was a volunteer at a local nature reserve, now closed, and I've been chairman of, and player with, Porthcawl Badminton Club since coming to South Wales. Language interests are maintained by being very much involved with Porthcawl - St Sébastien-sur-Loire (near Nantes) Twinning Association. My passion for birdwatching has taken me all over the world, while Margaret and I have entrusted ourselves to Saga's tender care on many visits to North Africa and Europe.

I conclude by thanking all of you who have bought my book. I do hope you enjoy it and that it will establish or renew links.

Floreat schola!

November 2020

SUBSCRIBERS

Ruth Ainley, Snaith

David Anderson, Chislehurst

Michael Baker, Birmingham

Paul Balderstone, Chichester

Margaret Ballard, Southampton

Alan J. Balmforth, Long Sutton

Clare Barlow, Ipswich

Melanie Barraclough, Netherlands

Charlotte Barrett, Huddersfield

John Battye, Ashford

Jean Luc & Monique Billet, France

Anna Bonet, Islington

Catherine Bonet, Greenwich

Jordi Bonet, Spain

Maria Luisa Bonet Carbonell, Spain

Ian Booth, Huddersfield

Gary Boothroyd, Oakham

Marie-Paule & Vincent Bouchaud, France

John Bradley, Australia

Simon Brett, Swindon

John Broadbent, Huddersfield

Roy B. & Jennifer A. Brook, Dumfries

Chris Brown, Huddersfield

Robin Brown, Bedale

Alan M.J. Bush, Longborough

Mike & Shirley Bush, Billingborough

Glyn Cannon, Huddersfield

Tony Cape, U.S.A.

Wanda Carradus, Beaumont Park

Linda T. Carter, Huddersfield

Graham Cliffe, Almondbury

Keith Crawshaw, Almondbury

David Gary Croft, Huddersfield

Ann Day, North Cornelly

Richard & Pam Dobbs, Porthcawl

Andrew Douglas, Huddersfield

Roger Dowling, Lymm

Terence Dowling, Aspatria

John H. Dyson, Norway

Linda Earnshaw, Huddersfield

Bobby & Mary Emment-Lewis, Porthcawl

Arlene Evans, North Cornelly

Ruth & Dai Evans, Porthcawl

Marjorie Faragher, Huddersfield

Bob Field, Huddersfield

Andrew Firth, Grimsby

Arthur & Mary Furze, Clevedon

Tracey A. Gallagher, Huddersfield

Karen George, Huddersfield

Nuria Gomez, Spain

J. Colin Graham, Huddersfield

Katie Graham, Denton

Richard & Nicole Green, Holmfirth

Peter Griffin, Knutsford

Helen Gunton, Jersey

Andrew Mark Haigh, Almondbury

David Haley, Huddersfield

Malcolm & Janet Hanbury, Porthcawl

Glyn & Pam Hardwicke, Porthcawl

Geoff Headey, Huddersfield

John Headey, Huddersfield

Martyn Hicks, Fixby

Heather Hinchliffe, Holmfirth

Chris Hirst, Norway

SUBSCRIBERS (continued)

Bryan Hopkinson, Huddersfield

Stephen Hoy, Holmfirth

Jane Hunt, Porthcawl

Scott Huson, U.S.A.

Connor Jackson, Huddersfield

Gareth Jenkins, Pontypridd

Keith Saunders & Cath Jones, Porthcawl

Martin Kain, Huddersfield

Revd Ron Lancaster, Kimbolton

Ralph Leach, Huddersfield

Ann Lee, Porthcawl

Ken Leech, Australia

Nick Leventis, West Bridgford

Matthew Littlewood, Oakes

Steven Littlewood, Australia

Neil Lomax, Switzerland

Andrea Longley, Bradford

Christopher M. Mann, Hitchin

Graham Megson, Huddersfield

Angela Melling & Bob Williams, Huddersfield

Graeme Milnes, Cardiff

Paul Moorhouse, London

Robert Moorhouse, Stockport

Nichola Mott, Wilmslow

Rachel Mumford, Hull

Lisa & Neil Murray, Dunfermline

Chris Newberry, Porthcawl

Ben Newton, Bristol

Patrick O'Brien, Huddersfield

Richard D. Oughton, Eastham, Wirral

Helen Paton, Enfield

Jennie Pearson, Dunfermline

Julie Pearson, Australia

Craig Pember, Huddersfield

David Pollard, Winchester

Michael Powner, Huddersfield

Kerry & Ann Preece, Porthcawl

Richard Preece, Porthcawl

Max Price, Islington

Martin Priestley, Lincoln

Walter Raleigh, Almondbury

Bernard Redfern, Meltham

Anne Rees, Swansea

Romilly Rees, Porthcawl

Rev. Pat Reid, Ilkley

Andrew Roberts, Huddersfield

Tim Roberts, Huddersfield

Alan Rosney, Cardiff

Richard Rowe, Porthcawl

Edward Royle, Leamington Spa

Judith Rushby, Sowerby Bridge

Simon Russell, Huddersfield

Jeffrey Sampson, Huddersfield

Brian Saunders, Porthcawl

Craig Saunders, London

Andrew Schofield, Huddersfield

Martin Sellens, Clacton on Sea

Phil Shaw, Huddersfield

John Oswin Smith, Saffron Walden

Brian Stahelin, Lepton

Hazel Stanton, Horsham

Charlie Starkey, U.S.A.

Barrie Stephens, Porthcawl

Hywel Stephens, London

SUBSCRIBERS (continued)

Roderick Sykes, France

Andrew Taylor, Bidford-on-Avon

Dennis Taylor, Chesterfield

Jack Taylor, Greetland

Jonathan D. Taylor, Huddersfield

Richard Teale, Holmfirth

Chris Temperton, Holmfirth

Simon Thackray, Halesworth

David Vivian Thomas, Porthcawl

Gordon Thomas, Bridgend

Dawn Tiplady, Huddersfield

Ann Turner, Huddersfield

Richard Wade, Huddersfield

Ben Walker, Huddersfield

Elaine Walsh, Huddersfield

Fanny Walshaw, Holmfirth

Mark Waring, Caerleon

Peter Warry, York

Gillian Webb, Urmston

Mike Wilkinson, Much Wenlock

Kathleen Willis, Farnborough

Brent Wilson, New Quay

John Wilson, Penarth

Sarah Wiper, Wakefield

Alan & Mary Wise, Almondbury

THE OLD ALMONDBURIANS' SOCIETY

*This book is published by the Old Almondburians' Society on
the occasion of the 100th anniversary of its formation in its
present form in 1920. The Society, which has members all
over the world, is a large fellowship of former pupils and staff
of King James's School (formerly King James's Grammar
School). Its objectives are to uphold the status of the school and
to link members to each other and to the school itself.*

*The author has been a highly supportive member of the Society
throughout his time at King James's and since his retirement
in 1996. He is a vice-President and former Chairman.*

1. King James's School, located in a beautiful setting in the Farnley Valley in Almondbury, near Huddersfield, West Yorkshire

2. The oldest buildings in the foreground date back to around 1760. Modern additions include a large Design Block, bottom right and Sports Hall, top left

3. The Grade II listed Schoolhouse was the residence of the school's headmaster until 1945. The author's office was upstairs to the right of the front door

4. The headmaster's garden, viewed from the window of the author's office. In past years the garden was often used in summer for open-air plays

5. The author's first view of the school as he walked each morning from Grasscroft, Almondbury. Prominent on the right is the Design Block of 1979/80.

6. Fenay Quad viewed from former Geography room N3. The memorial stone over the door is dated 1883.

7. Built originally as a classroom, the 'Big' later became the school Library and is now part of the Independent Learning Centre. The stained glass window bearing the school crest was by Art master Edward Akroyd.

8. A plaque recognises a major donation from children's author Michael Hardcastle MBE (King James's Grammar School 1944-51)

9. A relief of former headmaster Alfred Easther (1848-1876) on a wall of the Library

10. The Old Kitchen yard and entrance through which DAB entered school more than 7,000 times and where Jack Taylor waited to greet him on his final day

11. Steps leading down to the bus bay viewed from Big Tree Yard, through an area once known as 'the Bunk', where the arrival of the K.78 bus was patiently awaited

12. The present Principal's study in the old Schoolhouse, much changed since DAB occupied it when Acting Headmaster and where senior management team meetings were held

13. The magnificent school sports hall, where DAB trained with the Old Almondburians' soccer teams, where he played epic badminton matches against Peter Griffin and where his final assembly took place

14. *DAB is photographed with a happy group of school prizewinners in his final year. They are seated at the Big Tree, which features on numerous occasions in this diary.*

15. *The Old Dining Hall, now a classroom, dates back to 1848. The memorial tablet is to former headmaster Rev Alfred Easther, who died in 1880.*

16. Presentation Evening 1996 (left to right): Ben Newton (Head Boy), Laura Cliffe (Head Girl), Andrew Taylor, Clive Watkins, Pat Reid, David Bush, Chairman of Governors Jeffrey Woodward, Deputy Mayoress of Kirklees

17. Dave Bush's final Year 11 Latin group. Back row (left to right): Helen Riddalls, Kate Smith, Victoria Wilson, ClaireTodman, Emma O'Donnell, Louise Wood, Amanda Holgate, Carl Roberts. Middle row :Jacqueline Hinchliffe, Rachel Benson, Hannah Parry, David Bush, Ben Newton, Bernadette May, Laura Cliffe. Front row: Sarah Haigh, Catherine Shuttleworth, Kirsty Woodhouse, Rebecca Marsden, Clare Humphries